# THE PUGMIRE FAITH

## THE CUMBERLAND BLACKSMITH AND
## THE MOUNTAIN MEADOWS MASSACRE

D F HOUSTON

MANGO BOOKS

First edition published 2019

The right of D.F. Houston to be identified as the author
of this work has been asserted in accordance with
the Copyright, Designs & Patents Act 1988.

ISBN: 978-1-911273-49-3 (softcover)
ISBN: 978-1-911273-50-9 (ebook)


Published by

Mango Books
18 Soho Square
London W1D 3QL

www.MangoBooks.co.uk

# THE PUGMIRE FAITH

## THE CUMBERLAND BLACKSMITH AND THE MOUNTAIN MEADOWS MASSACRE

# THE PUGMIRE FAITH

## PART 1: JONATHAN PUGMIRE SR IN ENGLAND

## PART 2: JONATHAN PUGMIRE SR IN AMERICA

## PART 3: JONATHAN PUGMIRE SR: THE LATER YEARS

# ACKNOWLEDGEMENTS

My thanks begin with my father Michael Houston, who thought I would like to have a look at a handwritten document that dated back to the middle part of the nineteenth century which listed various birthdays and marriages. The document in question was accompanied by a large family Bible, given to my father by an elderly lady from the Lake District in Cumbria, northern England.

Without my being shown this document, you would not now be holding this book in your hands.

I would like to thank my publisher, Adam Wood of Mango Books, who was interested in this story and allowed me to write it with freedom and in my own style. He never pushed me in any direction, he only ever offered support.

I would also like to thank Professor John G. Turner, an esteemed lecturer and author of American religion and its history, who kindly took the time to look over my work and offer advice.

---

There was one other person I would like to thank, someone who encouraged me to write when I was a child, and I have done so ever since in one form or another – the late author Theresa Whistler, who I will always be grateful to.

When I was about seven-years-old, Theresa was invited to my primary school to hold a series of meetings with about a dozen children every Saturday, the plan being to eventually produce a book. The project was aimed at the older children who were preparing for secondary school. I wanted to join in, and after some persistence – even though I was four years younger – I was allowed into the group.

I can still remember the excitement of writing that I experienced back then, and I thank Theresa for letting me be part of that literary project.

# FOREWORD

One day in the spring of 2017 my father came over to where I live in the Lake District for our weekly get-together. On this occasion, he handed me an eight-page document and a large family Bible. Handwritten on the inside were details of the births and marriages of members of a family with a surname I had not heard before. The family members were all called Pugmire and had lived for generations in Cumbria, which is where I am writing this now.

The following was written on the inside of the front cover:

> Jonathan Pugmire Bought this Book
> December 5th 1879 From Martha Nichol of
> Sebergham Bridge Land for the sum of 10 Shillings
> Cousin to his wife Betsy Pugmire.

Now as someone who enjoys looking into the past and all things to do with genealogy, I was curious to find out more about these people.

After some research I managed to find records of the Pugmire family and their lives in 19th Century Cumbria. If it had ended at that point I would have been happy, having discovered something about the family and where, when and how they lived.

But this is where my research began in earnest. I looked further back in time with regard to Jonathan Pugmire, the person who had brought the Bible and who wrote the inscription back in December of 1879.

My research was successful, as I found information about his parents and grandparents. Now knowing his ancestors, I then worked forward to see if he had any other family members who had also lived in or around the same area.

He did.

Many of his relatives were born in Cumbria, where they

stayed and raised families of their own. One person, however, stood out.

There was a cousin who was also called Jonathan Pugmire, but who lived quite a different life.

This cousin, this Jonathan Pugmire, did not stay in the Lake District, or even in England.

Welcome, reader, to *The Pugmire Faith*.

# THE REAL PEOPLE
# OF THE BOOK

The following are some of the people who feature in this true story of one man's personal odyssey. There is a reason for introducing them at this point, at the beginning of the story; so that you will already know a little about them when they eventually appear in the book, and familiarity is better than confusion.

---

## Jonathan Pugmire Sr (1799-1876): The Lead Character

19th century English blacksmith and convert to Mormonism who travelled with his family to the United States of America.

## Thomas Cartwright (1814-1873): The Best Friend

Friend and co-worker of Jonathan Pugmire Sr, a fellow convert from Northern England who also relocated to the United States.

## Joseph Smith Jr (1805-1844):
## The Founder of a New Religion

The young man who, disappointed with the state of religion, founded his own and gave birth to what is known as Mormonism.

## Brigham Young (1801-1877):
## The Driving Force of the New Religion

Missionary and one-time powerful leader of the Latter Day Saints (the movement based on the teachings of Joseph Smith and Mormonism).

### Thomas Dunlop Brown (1807-1884): The Journal Keeper

Scottish convert to Mormonism and keeper of extensive journals regarding the emigrants who relocated from Britain to the United States in the mid part of the 19th century.

### William Law (1809-1892): The Whistle Blower

An excommunicated Mormon who published his concerns regarding certain aspects of Mormon faith in a short-lived newspaper.

### Sidney Rigdon (1793-1876): Friend of the Founder

One-time close friend of Joseph Smith and an early convert to Mormonism who would challenge for leadership.

### John Doyle Lee (1812-1877): The Military Leader

Friend of Joseph Smith and a Mormon, a military man who, as a leader, would be executed by a firing squad for his involvement in a massacre of travellers.

### Hyrum Smith (1800-1844): Brother of the Founder

Older brother of Mormon founder Joseph Smith and part of the Mormon movement.

### Isaac C Haight (1813-1886): A Military Man

Early convert to the Church of Jesus Christ of the Latter Day Saints and one of the leaders of the Mormon Militia who would be heavily involved in the Mountain Meadows Massacre.

### Philip Klingon Smith (1825-c.1881): The Polygamist

Early Mormon pioneer who was excommunicated after his involvement in the Massacre that took the lives of over 100 people.

## Jacob Hamblin (1819-1886): The Sensitive One

Mormon missionary and diplomat to the Native Americans who attempted to keep the peace between numerous groups of people at the height of conflict.

# INTRODUCTION

Now you have read a small part about some of the people who are important to this book, I can begin all the way back at the beginning.

------------

This true discourse of a man named Jonathan Pugmire Sr, a blacksmith born in the picturesque Lake District, begins right at the very end of the eighteenth century.

For those of you who are not familiar with the Lake District, it is situated in the county of Cumbria in northern England. This story starts over 200 years ago when Jonathan Pugmire was born in the county, although back then it was actually still known as Cumberland.

Pugmire would not remain in Cumberland for long, however. He had a mind to better himself and explore life away from the rural confines where he and his many cousins and second cousins were raised and expected to stay, to provide for the young and care for the old.

So it would transpire that, far from a quiet life in the green sleepy hills and the ancient lakes of northern England, Jonathan decided to leave his old life and family behind forever in his search for spiritual belonging.

This one single decision would lead to his involvement in incidents that would echo through history for several centuries to come and would affect more people then he could ever have possibly known.

What follows is a tale of drowning, imprisonment, emigration, religion, polygamy, war and mass murder.

------------

Now before I continue, let me make it clear that this is not a critique on any religion of any kind. Humans are afforded the freedom to believe what they wish to. That is the beauty of liberty.

No, dear reader, this is simply the historical tale of a real man who lived a real life.

With that in mind, enjoy this account of one man who lived 200 years before you and I, and who cared for family and friends and a life of contentment just as you reading this do now.

One other thing, and this is important: everything you are about to read actually took place.

Now if you are sitting comfortably, let me introduce you to a man who was born in the north of England and who died 4,000 miles away, far across the Atlantic Ocean, in Salt Lake City, Utah.

This is the true story of Englishman Jonathan Pugmire Sr.

# PART 1

# JONATHAN PUGMIRE SR
# IN ENGLAND

# THE EARLY LIFE OF JONATHAN PUGMIRE SR

*'An expert iron worker'*

---

Jonathan Pugmire came into this world on 28th March 1799 in the small Cumberland parish of Castle Sowerby to unmarried parents Jonathan Pugmire and Hannah Hetherington.

His father was born in 1765 and also hailed from Castle Sowerby. His mother, Hannah, was born in the nearby village of Sebergham in 1770.

Their son was christened as a member of the Church of England eight months after his birth, on 24th November 1799. This standard rite of passage for many 200 years ago took place at Raughton Head, a hamlet located approximately eight miles south of Carlisle and eleven miles north of Penrith, Cumberland.

On 6th July 1807, when Jonathan was eight-years-old, his mother Hannah married a man called Thomas Coulthard in Saint Saviour church, York. Not much is known about Thomas, except that he was 37 at the time of the marriage and had been born on 6th March 1770 in Wetheral, Cumberland. He died in the north of England in the 1840s.

By the dawning of the 1820s and now in his early twenties, Jonathan began looking for a vocation and decided to focus on his skills as a blacksmith, a trade he would be proud of and one that would serve him well in the future. It was around this time that he first experienced loss.

It was in 1823 that his father died. This would usually be seen as a milestone in sadness, although Jonathan had been raised for some time by his mother and stepfather. How close he was to his actual father is not known and perhaps, as I am about to explain, they did not have that great a connection.

Let me take you to the wedding of the young Jonathan Pugmire which had taken place three years earlier, on 7th October 1820.

Jonathan found himself standing nervously at the front of St Cuthbert's Church in Carlisle, looking over his shoulder to watch his intended, Elizabeth Barnes, walk slowly up the aisle whilst smiling somewhat coyly at the guests.

Let me tell you a bit about the bride. As I have stated, her name was Elizabeth. She was born on 15th October 1800 in Dalston, a small suburb situated on the outskirts of Carlisle, to George and Sarah Barnes. As we will see later, Elizabeth would prove to be a loyal wife and mother, but sadly would be dead before the end of 1846.

But there is something rather interesting relating to the marriage of Jonathan and Elizabeth in the Autumn of 1820; he used the surname 'Coulthard' rather than 'Pugmire', despite his father still being alive at the time. Why he chose to use the surname of his mother's second husband as his own for his wedding day is something of a mystery, and subsequent records show that Jonathan reverted back to his original surname of Pugmire.

# THE MORMON FOUNDER JOSEPH SMITH

*'When first I looked upon him, I was afraid;*
*but the fear soon left me'*

Joseph Smith

───────────────

Ten years after our protagonist Jonathan Pugmire married Elizabeth Barnes, a young man from the state of Vermont was offering disaffected Americans a new way of life where faith could be practiced with truth absolute.

The man in question was called Joseph Smith, and he had just successfully published his very own work entitled *The Book of Mormon*.

Now, before we get ahead of ourselves and look at this important event which took place across the Atlantic, we should first go all the way back to where it started for the founder of The Church of Jesus Christ of Latter Day Saints, Joseph Smith Jr.

───────────────

Joseph Smith Jr was born on 23rd December 1805 in the town of Sharon, Vermont to parents Joseph Smith Sr and Lucy Mack. His parents would have eleven children in total, with Joseph being the fifth.

His father, who would eventually go on to play an important role in the new faith formed by his son, tried his hand at numerous occupations. Finding himself the head of an expanding family, he spent some time working as, amongst other things, a teacher and a shopkeeper. Unfortunately, nothing seemed to provide him with more than moderate success.

It was mother Lucy who was responsible for instilling religious virtues into the younger members of the family as Joseph Sr, struggling to find work, originally had little interest in organized faith.

———————————

By 1817, when Joseph Jr was not yet twelve-years-old, the family had relocated to the state of New York and more specifically to the area that became known as the 'burned-over district'. It was Charles Grandison Finney (1792-1875), a prominent Presbyterian Minister at the time, who came up with this phrase after assuming that there was no member of the population in the central and western part of New York left to convert to a faith. In his view, New York State had been fully evangelised.

Joseph Sr brought his family here in an attempt to make a success of working in agriculture. They moved into a rented farm at Palmyra, New York State, and it was there when they found themselves in the midst of what would become known as the 'Second Great Awakening'.

# THE FIRST AND SECOND GREAT AWAKENING

What is the Second Great Awakening?, you may ask yourself.

This 'awakening' was a movement that began at the end of the Eighteenth Century which aimed to promote all things Protestant, just as the important First Awakening had set out to do in the 1730s. Before looking at the Second Awakening it is important to go back to the First.

---

The First Great Awakening (sometimes known as the Evangelical Revival) focused on teaching the Gospel across both England and the American colonies in the first half of the 18th Century. The focus returned back to the tradition of promoting Puritanism and placed emphasis on salvation, no matter a person's religious denomination.

It was not welcomed by some, who felt that unqualified fanatics now with a platform were able to teach whatever they wanted to the vulnerable listener. This awakening would give birth to the popular Methodist faith and bring together fellow Protestants who believed in tradition.

What is a Protestant?

According to the *Oxford English Dictionary*, a Protestant is 'a member or follower of any of the Western Christian Churches that are separate from the Roman Catholic Church in accordance with the principles of the Reformation, including the Baptist, Presbyterian, and Lutheran churches'.

In simple terms, a Protestant is someone who disagrees with certain aspects of the teachings of the Roman Catholic Church.

---

Some of the important people who were involved in this First Awakening included George Whitefield, John and Charles Wesley and Jonathan Edwards.

It all began in earnest in 1729 when Charles Wesley, who became a leader of the Methodist faith and is widely known for his many hymns, set up a group amongst fellow scholars called the Holy Club. His older brother John and friend George Whitefield soon became members.

It was Jonathan Edwards who was responsible for the greatest revival at this time, which took place between 1734 and 1735 in Northampton, Massachusetts.

---

The Second Great Awakening, favoured by Baptist and Methodist ministers, was very popular in 1817, the year Joseph Smith and his family relocated to New York from Vermont.

With regard to the philosophy of this awakening, focus was directed to the belief in the supernatural, amongst other things. Scepticism and rational views were disregarded and viewed with suspicion. This movement was a purposeful response to the emergence of the European Enlightenment Theory, which placed individual choice and free will as the basis of existence and development rather than an unseen force that controlled all things (deism).

An 11-year-old Joseph Smith would of course be impressionable at this time. A new ideology that questioned determinism was gathering momentum, and yet he found himself in an area of New York State where there was supposedly no-one left to convert.

What would happen to young Joseph Smith next, you may ask. Would he, a child, have an idea about how to change the direction of people's faith and bring it back to something which could be controlled?

"Yes," is the answer.

---

It was in 1820 that 14-year-old Joseph Smith Jr claimed that both God and Jesus appeared to him, telling him not to join any church as they had all failed to follow the general principles of Christianity. According to Smith, God explained that the one true church would be restored and he would be the one to facilitate this. This visitation would become known as the First Vision.

So what happened after this vision?

In 1823 Joseph claimed that he was visited several times by a messenger of God called Moroni, telling of an important record of events that took place in the Americas around two thousand years before involving someone called Mormon. In these visitations, Joseph was also supposedly told that these events were inscribed on heavy gold metal plates hidden under a hill near Palmyra, New York. Fortunately for the young Joseph Smith, this was right where the farm that his family had moved to in 1816 was located. According to the theology of the Church of Jesus Christ of Latter Day Saints, it was these plates that made up the foundation for the Book of Mormon.

---

Who, you might wonder, is Mormon?

Let me explain.

According to the Latter Day Saints, Mormon was a man born around 311AD and whose father was also called Mormon. It was when he was ten years of age that he was informed where he could find the sacred writings of the Nephite prophets.

The Book of Mormon explains that the Nephites were a group of people who left Jerusalem at the insistence of God and made their home in the Americas around 589BC.

When Mormon was eleven-years-old his father took him to Zarahemla (a large city in the Americas that as yet has never been authenticated as having existed). When he was 15, Jesus Christ visited him. At the age of 16 Mormon led the Nephites into many battles against the Lamanites.

In 362AD Mormon no longer wished to be leader of the Nephites due to their wickedness, but changed his mind on seeing how they were being beaten by the Lamanites.

While these events were taking place in the Americas, Mormon busied himself by collating words and information from important writers. He wrote down the most important of ideas he heard on metal plates, along with his own thoughts.

By 385AD the Nephites were completely destroyed and Mormon was killed, at which point his son Moroni found himself in charge of his father's work and subsequently ensured the safekeeping of the writings for many centuries to come.

———————

Let me go through with you the origin of the name The Church of Jesus Christ of Latter Day Saints. It was adopted by followers of Smith after his declaration that humans were experiencing the very last of days. Those who did not follow his beliefs called those who did 'Mormons'.

> And we are led to mingle our prayers with those of the Saints that have suffered the like treatment before us, whose souls are under the altar, crying to the Lord for vengeance upon those that dwell upon the earth. And we rejoice that the time is at hand, when the wicked who will not repent will be swept from the earth. (Joseph Smith).[1]

———————

The Church of Jesus Christ of the Latter Day Saints believe that it was on 22nd September 1823, upon a hill near his home in New York, that Joseph Smith first discovered the Golden Plates. This took place after an angel, who was actually Moroni, son of Mormon, had told him their location. Smith was instructed not to show anyone, not a single person, until the plates had been carefully translated from their original reformed Egyptian into English so that the followers could more easily understand:

1    *The Journal of Joseph: The Personal History of a Modern Prophet* (Lee Nelson, 1979).

> When first I looked upon him, I was afraid; but the fear soon left me. He called me by name, and said unto me that he was a messenger sent from the presence of God to me and that his name was Moroni... He said there was a book deposited, written upon gold plates, giving an account of the former inhabitants of this continent, and the sources from whence they sprang.[2]

Smith was not able to retrieve the plates on his first attempt, and would make several visits over several years to the hill that would become known as Cumorah until the moment was right. So it was that in September 1827 the Golden Plates were finally lifted from the ground.

In June 1829 Smith took his friends Martin Harris, Oliver Cowdery and David Whitmer (known as the Three Witnesses) into the woods at Fayette, New York. According to Mormonism, it was there that they all saw a vision of an angel holding the Golden Plates.

A few days after this Smith took eight people to a place near his parents' home in Palmyra to serve as witnesses, and showed all those gathered the Golden Plates. Known as the Eight Witnesses, their names feature in the appendix of the original 1830 publication of *The Book of Mormon*.

———————————

So how did Joseph Smith manage to translate the Golden Plates into English once they were lifted from the ground?

The Latter Day Saints explain that for several years after the discovery of the Golden Plates in 1827 Smith spent his time translating the words into what would eventually become the basis for *The Book of Mormon*. Smith himself explained that he was able to read the language and translate the plates with the use of a special stone, known as a seer stone. The Latter Day Saints believe that a seer stone is so special that only a few are selected to receive them by God. It is suggested that Joseph

2    *History of the Church, vol. 1*, by Joseph Smith, Deseret Book, 1976, pp. 11-12.

Smith put one of these stones into a hat he wore, and when placing the hat upon his head he could suddenly quite clearly read all of the strange unknown words that were inscribed onto the Golden Plates.

According to Mormon doctrine, after Smith had translated the plates he returned them back to the angel Moroni. In doing this, the followers of Mormonism would have to believe through faith in the words written by Joseph Smith. Evidence of his discovery, the Golden Plates, would now be gone forever.

The first edition of *The Book of Mormon* was published in March 1830.

To some, the origins of this religion may seem questionable, but it proved to be very popular, and not only where it began with Joseph Smith. It also gained momentum in Europe, especially in the working-class towns and cities in the north of England.

Our main character, Jonathan Pugmire, would soon become a convert himself.

# 4

# THE OHIO INCIDENT
# OF 1832

*'When I came to the door I was naked'*

Joseph Smith

---

The reaction to the publication of *The Book of Mormon* by the American public was not altogether welcoming.

One morning in 1832, while Joseph Smith and his friend and fellow Mormon Sidney Rigdon were staying at Hiram in Ohio, they found themselves in trouble with local residents who were not happy at this new doctrine telling them how to live their lives.

Smith would later record what happened when the angry mob came knocking and banging at his front door in *The History of the Church of Jesus Christ of Latter-day Saints*:

> On the 24th of March, the twins before mentioned, which had been sick of the measles for some time, caused us to be broken of our rest in taking care of them, especially my wife. In the evening I told her she had better retire to rest with one of the children, and I would watch with the sicker child. In the night she told me I had better lied down on the trundle bed, and I did so, and was soon after awakened by her screaming murder, when I found myself going out of the door, in the hands of about a dozen men...
>
> They then seized me by the throat and held on till I lost my breath. After I came to, as they passed along with me, about thirty rods from the house, I saw Elder Rigdon stretched out on the ground, whither they had dragged him by his heels. I supposed he was dead. I began to plead with them,

saying, 'You will have mercy and spare my life, I hope.'...

They ran back and fetched the bucket of tar, when one exclaimed, with an oath, 'Let us tar up his mouth;' and they tried to force the tar-paddle into my mouth; I twisted my head around, so that they could not... They then tried to force a vial into my mouth, and broke it in my teeth. All my clothes were torn off me except my shirt collar; and one man fell on me and scratched my body with his nails like a mad cat...

They then left me, and I attempted to rise, but fell again; I pulled the tar away from my lips, so that I could breathe more freely, and after a while I began to recover, and raised myself up, whereupon I saw two lights. I made my way towards one of them, and found it was Father Johnson's. When I came to the door I was naked, and the tar made me look as if I were covered with blood, and when my wife saw me she thought I was all crushed to pieces, and fainted...

———————————

Tarring and feathering was commonplace in 19th Century America, with public humiliation being seen as a way for a community to show their resentment of another person's actions. Author Richard Bushman described the incident in his book *Joseph Smith: Rough Stone Rolling:*

In early 1832, opposition took a violent turn. On Saturday, March 24, Joseph was dragged from his bedroom in the dead of night. His attackers strangled him until he blacked out, tore off his shirt and drawers, beat and scratched him, and jammed a vial of poison against his teeth until it broke. After tarring and feathering his body, they left him for dead. Joseph limped back to the Johnsons' house and cried out for a blanket. Through the night, his friends scraped off the tar until his flesh was raw.[3]

3    Richard Bushman: *Joseph Smith: Rough Stone Rolling*, p. 178.

The traumatic attack would have been very frightening indeed, although both Joseph Smith and Sidney Rigdon would not let what happened stop them from getting their message through to as many people as they could.

If anything Joseph, was invigorated and pushed forward with his belief.

Next stop - the rest of the World.

# 5

# MORMON MISSIONARIES

*'How can I go to preach in that land, which is so famed throughout Christendom for light, knowledge and piety'*

Heber C Kimball

———————

Clearly, the unfortunate events that dark night at Ohio in 1832 would not deter Joseph Smith and Sidney Rigdon nor the Latter Day Saints movement, and they both managed to leave what happened behind them.

According to Mormon doctrine, it was several years later, in 1835, when plans were first made to expand the Latter Day Saints' church overseas:

> And it shall come to pass that the righteous shall be gathered out from among all nations, and shall come to Zion, singing with songs of everlasting joy. (*The Doctrine and Covenants* 45:71)[4]

———————

In 1837 Mormon Elders Heber C Kimball and Orson Hyde were the two members of the Latter Day Saints who were sent overseas to England to act as missionaries.

Kimball was not filled with confidence, however, as he recorded in his journal:

4   *The Doctrine and Covenants* is the Church of Jesus Christ of the Latter Day Saints publication that details the revelations of Joseph Smith and other subsequent additions.

O, Lord, I am a man of 'stammering tongue,' and altogether unfit for such a work. How can I go to preach in that land, which is so famed throughout Christendom for light, knowledge and piety.'[5]

With doubts pushed aside, it was in April 1837 when the very first branch of a Mormon Congregation was founded in the northern English town of Preston, Lancashire.[6] This predates any other by ten years, and is actually the oldest functioning branch in the Mormon faith. According to the Latter Day Saints, some 1,500 people were baptized during this first venture across the Atlantic, which shows the popularity of the religion at the time.

The high number of converts to Mormonism in the north of England may be linked to the Industrial Revolution, which had peaked some years before. The introduction of contemporary machines, especially in the North of England, would have left people questioning their place and requirement in the factory environment. Without work there would be no money, and without money there would be no food.

The missionaries from far across the ocean who came offering a new life would be appealing to those people who were unsure of their future, and the future of their children.

———————

Following the success of Mormon Elders Kimball and Hyde, a group of missionaries were carefully selected to return to England. It was on this journey that the chosen were required to build the Church of Mormonism, both figuratively and in actuality. Those selected for this particular mission were known collectively as the Quorum of the Twelve Apostles.

5    Heber C. Kimball's *Journal* (1882), p. 10.
6    The fact that the first branch set up in Preston interests me as I know the place and its history, having lived there twice: once as a secondary school student and then again ten years later when studying for a degree at the University.

And next spring let them depart to go over the great waters, and there promulgate my gospel, the fulness thereof, and bear record of my name. (*The Doctrine and Covenants* 118:4)

———————————

# 6

# THE QUORUM OF THE TWELVE APOSTLES

*'Surely this is an important day to behold'*

Wilford Woodruff Sr

---

So it was that in 1839 the first Quorum of the Twelve Apostles (second only in importance at the time to the founder Joseph Smith), without money or provisions, arrived on British shores to follow Joseph Smith's instructions.

It is interesting to note that the members who had been chosen for the task actually consisted of eleven people and not twelve. This was because the last place had not been filled when the mission began.

---

The members who were part of the very special Quorum included:

## Brigham Young

Brigham Young was sent by Joseph Smith to serve the Mormon faith overseas. Preaching the new religion seemed to come easy to Young as he led the faith from the missionary headquarters in Preston.

Following the death of Joseph Smith, Young would be elected leader of the Latter Day Saints and take fellow believers to the state of Utah. 'Salt Lake City' in Utah, now synonymous with Mormonism, was named by Brigham Young.

Eighteen years after his missionary trip to England, Young would play a pivotal role in what would become known as the Mountain Meadows Massacre. This event will be discussed in detail later on in the book.

In 1876 he would meet with Jonathan Pugmire, who was at this time in failing health. Young himself died the following year at Salt Lake City.

### John Taylor

Born in Westmoreland (modern day Cumbria), close to where Jonathan Pugmire was born, Taylor would go on to become the third President of The Church of Jesus Christ of Latter Day Saints. Taylor would be the only elected President who was born outside of the United States.

John Taylor was also one of the few people who were present when Mormon founder Joseph Smith and his brother Hyrum were murdered in 1844.

The Mormon Fundamentalist Movement, who follow the teachings of Joseph Smith and Brigham Young, cite John Taylor as the person who received what became known as the 1886 Revelation, said to have taken place on 27th September that year, which stated that plurality in marriage was acceptable.

### Wilford Woodruff Sr

Connecticut-born Woodruff Sr would marry at least nine times and become the fourth President of The Church of Jesus Christ of Latter Day Saints.

A keen diarist, Woodruff kept detailed accounts of his life within the Latter Day Saints. The following entry was made on 7th July 1839:

> Following the setting apart of the Twelve for their mission to England and the instructions of the First Presidency to them. Reflections. Surely this is an important day to behold a quorum of Twelve Apostles.

Woodruff believed that the Second Coming was imminent

and his sermons would focus on the destruction of the Earth. In 1880, many years after his missionary across the water, he detailed in his journal a revelation that had come to him:

> The hour of God's judgement is fully come and shall be poured out without measure upon the wicked... Prepare ye for the coming of the Son of man, which is nigh at the door. No man knoweth the day nor the hour; but the signs of both heaven and earth indicate His coming, as promised by the mouths of my disciples. The fig trees are leaving and the hour is nigh.[7]

Wilford died in San Francisco at the grand age of 91.

## George A Smith

George was born in New York and was a cousin of Joseph Smith. At the age of 15 he was baptized into the Church of Jesus Christ of the Latter Day Saints, his parents having been baptized eight months before.

He was made a member of the Quorum of the Twelve Apostles on 26th April 1839 along with Wilford Woodruff.

Smith followed Brigham Young to Utah after the death of Joseph Smith, and as a Mormon pioneer set up a community along with other Mormon followers. The community they built together was called Parowan, and would be the place where, in 1852, an 11-year-old child called John Pugmire would be shot and killed.

Smith would also play an important role in the massacre that took place in 1857 at Mountain Meadows.

He married seven times and fathered some 20 children before his death in 1875 in Salt Lake City.

During one sermon Smith explained his position with regard to multiple marriages:

---

7    Erickson, Dan (1998). *'As a Thief in the Night': The Mormon Quest for Millennial Deliverance.* Salt Lake City, Utah: Signature Books (p189).

We breathe the free air, we have the best looking men and handsomest women, and if [non-Mormons] envy us our position, well they may, for they are a poor, narrow-minded, pinch-backed race of men, who chain themselves down to the law of monogamy, and live all their days under the dominion of one wife. They ought to be ashamed of such conduct, and the still fouler channel which flows from their practices; and it is not to be wondered at that they should envy those who so much better understand the social relations.[8]

## Willard Richards

Born in Massachusetts, when Richards was 4-years-old he injured his head after a fall. This accident made physical activity difficult and so he grew up focusing on education and educating others.

It was in 1836 that his cousin Brigham Young introduced him to *The Book of Mormon*.

Willard would be one of those who found themselves in jail along with founder Joseph Smith several years later.

## William Smith

William was the younger brother of founder Joseph Smith and was present when the Golden Plates were revealed. Joseph allowed his younger brother to touch them, although looking at them was forbidden.

William Smith was not the original choice to be a member of the Quorum. His brother ordered that he replace Phineas Young, the elder brother of future leader Brigham Young. This decision was not without criticism.

Oliver Cowdery and David Whitmer, two of the three Witnesses who, according to Mormon faith, were present with Joseph Smith when the Golden Plates were discovered in 1829, had their own views on the inclusion of William Smith as one of

8   *Journal of Discourses*, Vol 3, p291.

the Quorum. They are recorded as saying that the selection was

> contrary to our feelings and judgment, and to our deep mortification ever since.[9]

After the death of his brother, tensions grew between William Smith and future leader Brigham Young. This resulted in William being excommunicated from the Church.

He died in Clayton County, Iowa, at the age of 82.

## John E Page

John Edward Page was born in New York and was invited by Joseph Smith to join the Quorum of the Twelve Apostles. After the death of Smith in 1844 he put himself forward as the next leader, although this did not materialize. The Church at this time was under the leadership of Brigham Young, and the claims of Page to be leader were dismissed.

Page would go on to suggest that Joseph Smith was a 'fallen prophet'. He died in October 1867 in Sycamore, Illinois.

---

It was in April 1840 when the Mormon missionaries eventually made their way to the church headquarters in Preston, where fellow member of the Twelve Brigham Young assumed control of the Mormon Church in England. A meeting was held and the suggestion to publish *The Book of Mormon*, a hymn book and accompanying monthly periodical[10] for the British followers was agreed upon.

---

9    LDS Church History Library.
10   *Latter-day Saints' Millennial Star.*

# 7

# THE PUGMIRE FAMILY
# IN LIVERPOOL

*'About the age of 14 years I went to serve an apprenticeship
at blacksmithing in the establishment owned by
the Grand Junction Railway Company'*

Jonathan Pugmire Jr

---

It is not known whether Jonathan Pugmire attended any of
the Mormon gatherings held in Preston, although he was in the
area at the time and the following year he would indeed become
a member of the Church of the Latter Day Saints.

By 1841 he had secured employment as a foreman to the
blacksmiths with the Grand Junction Railway Company, and
had left Cumberland for Liverpool. The 1841 census taken on
Sunday 6th June records Jonathan as living on the city's Myrtle
Street with his wife Elizabeth and their five children.

On 14th November 1841, Pugmire, Elizabeth and their son
Jonathan Jr were baptized in the River Mersey and became
members of the Church of Jesus Christ of Latter Day Saints.
Elder John James baptized them, and another Elder named
George L Adams conducted a confirmation.

Jonathan Pugmire Jr's personal recollections of the event can
be found in a 1947 book by Kate B Carter called *Heart Throbs
of the West*:

> I was born on the 7th day of December A.D. 1823, in the
> city of Cumberland, England. At an early age, moved with
> my father and his family to Liverpool. About the age of 14

years I went to serve an apprenticeship at blacksmithing in the establishment owned by the Grand Junction Railway Company, Crown Street, Edge Hill, Liverpool, my father being foreman of the shop. I worked until the company moved their establishment to Crew S. Cheshire on the 14th day of November 1841. I and my father were baptised in the River Mersey into the Church of Jesus Christ of Latter -day Saints by Elder John James and confirmed by Elder George L. Adams, and became members of the Liverpool Branch of said Church, emigrating to Utah in 1848'.[11]

This baptism would prove to be a turning point; Jonathan Pugmire Sr[12] and his family were now committed members of the Mormon faith, with Pugmire Sr becoming the leader of a small number of Mormons in the Crewe area.[13]

---

It did not take long for the family to immerse themselves into the new religion that was finding its feet in Liverpool, and become ardent followers of *The Book of Mormon*. The travelling missionaries from overseas offered a new life in America, and several years later Jonathan Pugmire Sr would indeed cross the vast Atlantic Ocean and eventually arrive at a city called Nauvoo, Illinois, before heading west to the state of Utah.

The journey would not be an easy one, however. Before reaching his destination, Jonathan will find himself involved in a fatal drowning, a brief prison sentence on an accusation of manslaughter and the death of his wife.

---

11 Chapter 'The Pioneer Blacksmith of West Jordan' in *Heart Throbs of the West* by Kate B Carter.

12 To differentiate between Pugmire and his son of the same name, from this point on the name suffixes "Senior" and "Junior" will be used.

13 *The Cheshire Tragedy* by Ardis E Parshall (1843).

# 8

# THE DROWNING
# OF MRS CARTWRIGHT

*'Damn you, I'll dip ye!'*

Sarah Cartwright

---

It was a dark, cold night on 23rd November 1843 when a young, heavily-pregnant woman named Sarah Cartwright met her unexpected death in a river in the north of England.

She was found standing almost upright in the river the following day when the sun came up. By this time the water had receded, and her semi-naked body was left for all to see. This was a strange sight indeed; what had taken place, and why had she drowned?

The baptism of her husband Thomas Henry Cartwright into the Church of the Latter Day Saints by the man who is the subject of this book only a few weeks earlier may answer that question.

Earlier in 1843 the Pugmire family had moved to Crewe through Jonathan's work, as the Grand Junction Railway Company had relocated there from Liverpool. One of the blacksmiths under his command was 29-year-old Thomas Cartwright who, along with his young family, had also recently left Liverpool and moved the fifty miles or so to the railway town of Crewe in order to find employment.

---

On the evening of 6th November 1843 pregnant Sarah Cartwright, now in her early thirties, was at home at Crewe with her three young children, Jane, Sarah Ann and Ellen. Becoming ever more frustrated with the absence of her husband, Sarah found herself wondering when he would decide to make a return.

At that same moment, Jonathan Pugmire Sr, now officially a Mormon Elder in the area, had just finished baptising Thomas Cartwright into the Church of the Latter Day Saints in the Valley Brook near the homes of both families.

Such an event would not please Sarah Cartwright, who was not persuaded by the emergent Mormon movement. For the moment, however, she was frustrated that her husband was missing and so left the house, wandering down the street to the Pugmires' front door and knocking upon it several times.

When Elizabeth Pugmire opened the door and said she had no idea where Tom was, Sarah turned and began making her way home, only to see her husband, wet hair and all, walking towards her alongside Jonathan Pugmire Sr.

Furious, Sarah shouted at them, "Damn you, I'll dip ye!" According to testimonies given later, she was swearing at them both in anger, and promised revenge on Pugmire Sr and his family for turning her husband into a follower of the new religion.

Despite his wife's views about the Mormon Church, Thomas continued to make many visits to the Pugmire house to pray and to learn more about the faith. Expressing her disdain for the baptism Tom had undergone, Sarah is reported as saying, "I hope to God, if ever I am such a fool, that I'll be drowned in the attempt!"

It was eighteen days later, on 24th November 1843, that the lifeless, semi-naked body of Sarah Cartwright would be recovered from a nearby river.

# 9

# A FULL IMMERSION

*'I am very sorry; and as my conduct is known to all this
neighborhood, I do not wish to have my baptism public.'*

Sarah Cartwright

---

Despite her scepticism, it seems that in the fortnight following
her husband's initiation into Mormonism Sarah Cartwright at
least made an attempt to learn more about the faith.

She listened to her Thomas excitedly talk at length about the
truth of the words within the Mormon text which he had been
introduced to by Jonathan Pugmire Sr; she eventually decided
to visit Pugmire to hear for herself. The Elder must have been
somewhat persuasive, for Sarah Cartwright returned several
times over the days which followed and, fearful of incurring
anger from God, agreed to join her husband and be baptised
into the Church of Latter Day Saints.

What happened next is not quite clear. The records kept by
the Mormon Church describe Sarah visiting the Pugmire house
on one further occasion:

> Mrs. Pugmire talked with her, reminding her of her harsh
> expression. She confessed all, and said, "I am very sorry;
> and as my conduct is known to all this neighborhood, I do
> not wish to have my baptism public, but to have it done
> privately; and I wish no female to accompany me to the
> water but you.[14]

So it was that on the evening of 23rd November 1843 pregnant
Sarah was taken down to the river by her husband Thomas,

---

14    Volume 6 Chapter 7 of *The History of the Church of Jesus Christ of Latter Day Saints.*

Jonathan Pugmire Sr, his wife Elizabeth and a man called James Moore. Jonathan was confident, having already baptised between eight and ten people in the same river.

This is where it goes wrong.

A large amount of rain had fallen that day, and the river had overflowed and was filled right up to the top of the banks. Pugmire mused as the water sped along before him. He crouched down and put his hand in the water before feeling the side of the bank to see if it was secure. Shaking his hands, he turned to the others and exclaimed that the baptism would still go ahead.

He carefully led Sarah down the side of the bank into the cold, dark water. After managing to stand together in the water and perform the ceremony with the other three watching from the side, they begin to climb out. It was at this moment when they suddenly lost their footing and, despite desperately trying to hold on to something, disappeared under the water.

When Thomas saw his wife disappear into the water he jumped in without a moment's thought. He managed to grab hold of her petticoat, but it was not enough to hold on to her and she vanished under the water as he continued to drift down the river, still grasping that one piece of clothing in his hand.

James Moore, the other witness on the bank, managed to grab hold of Jonathan Pugmire Sr by his hair. With the help of Mrs Pugmire, they were able to pull him out of the river and to safety.

Moore then ran back to Crewe to fetch help. He returned minutes later with a man called George Knowlen and both men scoured the river. It was further down where they saw a shivering Thomas Cartwright, desperately trying to keep his head above the water whilst holding onto a tree.

Sarah was discovered in the river the next day, 200 yards away standing upright. The water had by this time receded some two feet, leaving her lifeless body exposed.

# 10

# ARREST AND TRIAL

*'You have been most culpable in not having examined the brook in which you had proposed to observe your baptismal ceremony.'*

Justice J Wightman

---

It would not take long for justice to catch up with Jonathan Pugmire Sr:

> On Pugmire reaching home, a Church of England minister had him arrested and dragged from his family the same evening, and kept in custody of a constable until a coroner's inquest was held on the body of the deceased.[15]

Following the inquest both Pugmire and Thomas Cartwright were taken to Chester, where they spent six weeks in jail awaiting trial.

On 9th December *The Leeds Intelligencer* published the following article, which described what happened on the day Sarah Cartwright drowned and why the pair found themselves in jail accused of manslaughter:

> Strange Occurrence – The Mormonites have been performing a tragedy at Crewe, which has caused a great sensation in that quarter. The wife of a smith, employed on the railway company's works at Crewe, went, in company with her husband and the resident Mormonite priest between eight and nine o'clock on the 23rd to be baptised in a brook in the neighbourhood. The brook

---

15    Volume 6 Chapter 7 of the *History of the Church of Jesus Christ of Latter Day Saints.*

was much swollen with the late rains, and the stream very rapid; the bank gave way, and the woman and the priest were precipitated into the brook. The priest saved himself; but the woman was drowned. Drags, &c, were used immediately on the alarm being given, but the body was not found till noon on Friday. The priest was arrested to await the result of the inquest, which was held on Saturday; when it appeared from the evidence of several of the deceased's neighbours, that she had experienced some ill usage from her husband, in consequence of her not being willing to be baptized; and that she went unwillingly, in consequence of his threats. The Coroner, upon this, caused the husband to be taken into custody, and a verdict of manslaughter was returned against both husband and priest, who were both committed to Chester Castle. The deceased was the mother of three children, and was again nearly seven months advanced in pregnancy. Both the parties committed were fellow workmen. It appeared that preparatory to baptizing the deceased she was stripped, though the night was cold, almost to a state of nudity, having on only a flannel shirt and petticoat. She slipped from the hands of the parties, Thomas Cartwright, her husband, and Jonathan Pugmire, the priest, and was carried down by the Coppenhall Brook, and perished about 300 yards from the spot where they were, about half a mile from Crewe, on the Chester line of railway. The inquest was held before Mr. Roskell, of Knutsford. The general impression is that the husband was actuated by a conscientious, but mistaken motive. She refused to be baptized if a third party were not present.[16]

Despite the accusation of manslaughter hovering over his head, Jonathan Pugmire Sr was still, at this time, in good spirits. He would later explain that while in jail he had received a vision explaining how everything would be fine, and innocence would be shown. This vision gave Jonathan confidence that both he and Thomas would be acquitted and released from the cells at Chester jail.

Next for them both would be the trial.

16    *The Leeds Intelligencer*, 9th December 1843 page 7.

The said trial of Thomas Cartwright and Jonathan Pugmire Sr for manslaughter began in front of a full courtroom at the Winter Assizes[17] in Chester on Tuesday, 2nd January 1844 at exactly nine o'clock.

In charge of the trial was Mr Justice William Wightman. Notes taken at the Assizes state the following:

> Jonathan Pugmire, blacksmith (an officiating minister of the Mormonites, commonly called Latter-day Saints), and Thomas Cartwright, blacksmith also, were placed at the bar, charged with the offence of killing and slaying one Sarah Cartwright, at Monks Coppenhall, in the vicinity of Crewe.

The prosecutor, Mr Townsend, told the courtroom that the prisoners were responsible for 'felonious killing'. Whether it was planned or a tragic accident, he explained, would be for the jury to decide.

The practice of the Latter Day Saints followers to carry out immersion during baptism was discussed during the trial. It was clear as proceedings continued that the new Mormon religion left many questioning exactly what it all meant, and why people were beginning to follow it with such fervour.

Because the prosecutor could not gather his witnesses nor offer any evidence for premeditation or negligence, Justice Wightman told the jury to acquit the accused, which they duly did. Mr Townsend explained he would make sure the witnesses appeared and asked for a retrial. The judge stated that no further trial would take place as it would then be a case of *autrefois acquit* (formerly acquitted).

In his summing up, Justice Wightman told Thomas Cartwright,

---

17  The word 'assizes' has several meanings including to sit, session and assist. The court of assizes which periodically gathered and dealt with serious criminal activity was replaced in 1972 by the permanent Crown Court.

It is my duty to remark, although with your particular
tenets I have nothing to do, you have been most culpable in
not having examined the brook in which you had proposed
to observe your baptismal ceremony. The pain which you,
Thomas Cartwright, I hope have experienced from the
dreadful consequences which have ensued will be a warning
to you hereafter.

Having found freedom once more, it would not be long before
both Jonathan Pugmire Sr and his friend Thomas Cartwright
decided to leave England for pastures new in the United States
of America, and all memories of what happened that dark night
in Chester would be left behind them.

But there would be more problems to come for both Jonathan
and his friend Thomas.

# PART 2

## JONATHAN PUGMIRE SR
## IN AMERICA

# 11

# THE PUGMIRE FAMILY LEAVE LIVERPOOL

## 'Boarding the Isaac Allerton'

---

Admiring the success of Brigham Young's Mormon missionary in England, Jonathan Pugmire Sr, happy to be free of any culpability regarding the death of his friend's wife by drowning, came to a decision. He would leave the comfortable familiarity of the north of England and head for America.

As for Thomas Cartwright himself, not long after the death of Sarah and before leaving England he married again, in Liverpool, to a woman from Dublin named Jane Allen.

Thomas would, in time, go on to marry for a third time, to a woman who came from Wigan named Catherine Beswick. He would eventually die in Beaver County, Utah on 9th January 1873 at the age of 58. But this is far from the last you will hear of Thomas Cartwright.

---

Back to Jonathan Pugmire. Maybe it was a higher calling, or perhaps the enticement of moving to a land where anything was possible that drove him to his decision to emigrate, but whatever the reason, on 6th February 1844 the Pugmire family packed up all their belongings, shut the door to their humble terraced house one final time and found themselves standing together at the Liverpool docks as they waited to board a boat for America.

They would travel on the *Isaac Allerton*.[18] Shipping records

---

18  Named after one of the people on board the *Mayflower*'s voyage in 1620, the *Isaac Allerton* sank off the coast of Florida on 28th August 1856.

taken at the time show that there were 60 passengers aboard during that voyage, and the Pugmire family made up eight of them:

Jonathan Pugmire Sr aged 44
Elizabeth Pugmire (Barnes) aged 43
Jonathan Pugmire Jr aged 20
Sarah Pugmire aged 17
Joseph Hyrum Pugmire aged 10
Elizabeth Pugmire aged 9
John Pugmire aged 3
Hannah Pugmire aged 1

Jonathan and Elizabeth's eldest son George Pugmire, who was 22 at the time, decided to stay in Liverpool with his wife, a woman called Jane Russell.

It is hard to imagine just how big a decision this was for the Pugmire family, to leave all they knew behind to make the great journey across the ocean. But it would seem that the enticement of being part of a new religious movement was something that Jonathan could not ignore.

Some of the younger Pugmire children were undoubtedly excited. It was an adventure after all. Transport, however, was somewhat slower than it is now though and the crossing of the Atlantic took quite some time.

# 12

# CROSSING THE ATLANTIC

*'So loud and tedious a journey'*

John Moon

---

It would take many weeks before the Pugmires finally arrived in the United States.

Leonard Arrington, the first church historian of the Latter Day Saints, described what life was like for emigrants such as the Pugmires when crossing the Atlantic:

> The companies arose at an early hour, made their beds, cleaned their assigned portion of the ship, and threw the refuse overboard. At seven they assembled for prayer, after which breakfast was had. All were required to be in their berths ready for retirement at eight o'clock. Church services were held morning and evening of each day, weather permitting. Many of the companies had excellent choirs which sang for the services. During the time of passage, which occupied something like a month, concerts, dances, contests, and entertainments of various types were held. Schools were held almost daily for both adults and children. The classes were particularly popular with Scandinavians who learned English en route.[19]

In 1840 John Moon, captain of the *Britannia*, had written to a William Clayton about the voyage he had recently undertaken from England to New York. Clayton then reproduced it for Brigham Young and Willard Richards, who were still active missionaries in England:

19  *Great Basin Kingdom* (1958), 103.

Bro Jno Moon writes – N York July 22 – I feel glad to find my feet upon the Land of Joseph after so loud and tedious a journey; we have had a very long voyage but quite as short.[20]

In 1863 Charles Dickens visited the London docks and came across a ship called the *Amazon* which contained Latter Day Saints emigrants preparing to leave the for a new life in America. The novelist recounted his experience in his book *The Uncommercial Traveller*:

Nobody is in an ill temper, nobody is the worse for drink, nobody swears an oath or uses a coarse word, nobody appears depressed, nobody is weeping, and down upon the deck, in every corner where it is possible to find a few spare feet to kneel, crouch, or lie in, people in every unsuitable attitude for writing, are writing letters.[21]

Dickens had expected to find a group of people he could readily criticise, but after seeing the passengers he changed his mind:

Had come aboard this emigrant ship to see what eight hundred Latter-day Saints were like... Indeed, I think it would be difficult to find eight hundred people together anywhere else, and find so much beauty and so much strength and capacity for work among them.[22]

Jonathan Pugmire Sr was certainly strong; he had overcome the accidental drowning of his friend's wife and the subsequent trial, and the decision to take his family and leave the country he was born and raised in.

---

20  19th August 1840.
21  Page 445.
22  Page 446.

# 13

# AT NEW ORLEANS

*'Preparing to cross the Mississippi River'*

---

After 45 long days at sea aboard the *Isaac Allerton*, Jonathan Pugmire, the blacksmith from Cumberland, his wife and their children finally arrived at the bustling port in the city of New Orleans.

After gathering their possessions and disembarking, the Pugmire family found themselves standing together surveying the shores of the imposing Mississippi river. They boarded a large steamer and began their journey down the river, the standard route for all newly converted Mormon emigrants. They would finally arrive at a city called Nauvoo in Illinois on 5th April 1844, but would not stay here for long, however, as events about to take place there would alter their original plans and change everything not just for the Pugmires, but for all who followed Joseph Smith and his new faith.

# 14

# THE NAUVOO EXPOSITOR

*'I told him that if they wanted peace they could
have it on the following conditions.'*

William Law

---

On 7th June 1844 the first and only edition of a newspaper
called the *Nauvoo Expositor* was published from premises in the
Illinois city. Nauvoo was given its name by Mormon founder
Joseph Smith in 1840, and in Hebrew means 'Beautiful place'.

Mormons had first arrived there at the end of 1839, to what
was a town then known as Commerce, and bought the land,
quickly turning the town into a city.

Not all settlers here would be happy with Mormonism and
specifically Joseph Smith's rhetoric on theology, economics and
politics, and after breaking away these 'renegades' grouped
together to publish the *Nauvoo Expositor*. This, as you will see,
would ultimately lead to the death of Mormon founder Joseph
Smith.

---

It was former friend of Smith named William Law who decided
to produce the newspaper, after after being excommunicated
from the Mormon Church. Law decided to expose Joseph Smith
for, amongst other things, his belief of having multiple wives. As
you will see shortly, he did have personal experience of such a
view.

According to William Law's wife Jane,[23] Joseph Smith had

---

23   Jane Silverthorn (1815-1882).

made several advances towards her requesting marriage. She explained that Joseph had "asked her to give him half her love; she was at liberty to keep the other half for her husband."[24] Jane dismissed the requests, and on 14th April 1844 she and her husband found that they were no longer associated with the church.

From once being a prominent member of the Mormon Church and part of the First Presidency,[25] William Law now found himself on the outside and could not keep his opposing views of certain practices to himself any longer. Like a kettle boiled, William was ready to let off steam.

---

Law's feelings did not go unnoticed and many leading members of the Mormon Church including Hyrum, Joseph Smith's brother, visited Law and asked him to reconsider his position. On 13th May 1844 Sidney Rigdon, on behalf of the Church of the Latter Day Saints, met with Law in hope of bringing peace.

About the meeting, Law recorded the following in his diary:

> I told him that if they wanted peace they could have it on the following conditions. That Joseph Smith would acknowledge publicly that he had taught and practised the doctrine, and that he should own the whole system (revelation and all) to be from Hell.[26]

As the Church of the Latter Day Saints would obviously not agree with this, Law and seven other people set about producing a newspaper that would shame the skewed morality that existed within the Church. It would expose what was happening in the Mormon community at Nauvoo and be called the *Nauvoo Expositor*.

---

24  *Wife No 19* by Ann Eliza Young, 1875, page 61.
25  The governing body of the Latter Day Saints.
26  Diary of William Law, 13th May 1844.

# 15

# THE FIRST EDITION

*'I hereby certify that Hyrum Smith did, (in his office,) read to me a certain written document, which he said was a revelation from God.'*

William Law

---

So it was that on 7th June 1844 that the first edition of the *Nauvoo Expositor* was published. This edition consisted of only four pages, and was for the most part made up of poetry and marriage notifications. However, there was one piece of writing which was designed to expose the church's conduct that lit the fuse.

The article in question focused on Joseph Smith's polygamy (an open secret within the Mormon community) and the accepting plurality of wives. Statements were reproduced explaining how Joseph Smith taught a revelation that some men could have more than one wife.

On page two of the *Expositor*, William Law published the following affidavit:

> I hereby certify that Hyrum Smith did, (in his office,) read to me a certain written document, which he said was a revelation from God, he said that he was with Joseph when it was received. He afterwards gave me the document to read, and I took it to my house, and read it, and showed it to my wife, and returned it next day. The revelation (so called) authorized certain men to have more wives than one at a time, in this world and in the world to come. It said this was the law, and commanded Joseph to enter into the law and also that he should administer to others. Several

other items were in the revelation, supporting the above doctrines.[27]

William's wife Jane gave the following statement which was included in the *Expositor*:

> I certify that I read the revelation referred to in the above affidavit of my husband, it sustained in strong terms the doctrine of more wives than one at a time, in this world, and in the next, it authorized some to have to the number of ten, and set forth that those women who would not allow their husbands to have more wives than one who should be under condemnation before God.[28]

It was the heavy reporting of polygamy that led to the end of the newspaper after only one single solitary edition, and also to the end of their lives for Joseph Smith and his brother Hyrum.

27  *Nauvoo Expositor* Vol 1, Friday 7th June 1844, page 2.
28  The *Expositor* states that Robert D Foster was witness to this statement when it was given on 4th May 1844.

# 16

# THE REACTION
# OF JOSEPH SMITH

*'I could not even suspect men of being such fools'*

William Law

---

So how did Joseph Smith react to the publication of the *Nauvoo Expositor*?

He was furious about it, and that is putting it mildly. After reading what had been printed, Smith ordered that a City Council meeting be organised. This took place on 8th June 1844, and he demanded the editors be put on trial for what had been written in the newspaper. The gathered Council agreed that the *Expositor* was a public nuisance, and Smith ordered that the *Nauvoo Expositor* premises be destroyed, by fair means or foul.

So it was, that just as the sun was setting on Monday 10th June 1844, that selected police officers entered a building in downtown Nauvoo and climbed the stairs to the second floor where the *Nauvoo Expositor* presses and equipment were. The City Marshall John P Greene[29] waved a piece of paper signed by Joseph Smith, who was Acting Mayor at the time, that authorized the destruction of the printing press and any equipment or superfluous copies of the *Expositor* that were found inside the building.

As Greene got to the second floor he found that the door was locked. One of the Higbee brothers, who stood outside,

---

29   John Portineus Greene (1793-1844) was the chief of police in Nauvoo and went with the Smith brothers to the jail at Carthage. He died of poisoning in September of 1844 during the Succession Crisis, when candidates stepped forward after the death of Joseph Smith to lead the Mormon Church.

initially refused them entry. After Greene claimed he would not demolish the building as he was asked to do, Higbee conceded and opened the door.

Also inside the room was Charles Foster who, along with the Higbees, watched somewhat helplessly as the police began carrying away the equipment from their premises. Once outside, the printing press was destroyed in the street with a sledgehammer and any copies of the newspaper found in the building burned.

William Law was in the nearby town of Carthage, Illinois at the time, and did not believe that the *Nauvoo Expositor* building would actually be attacked. In his diary he wrote:

> I was told that our press would be destroyed, but I did not believe it. I could not even suspect men of being such fools, but to my utter astonishment tonight upon returning from Carthage to Nauvoo I found our press had actually been demolished by Marshall J P Green, by order of the Mayor and the City Council.[30]

Following this destruction no further publication of the *Expositor* was ever made.

The actions of Joseph Smith and his elected officers did not go down well with the public. This is evident from an 11th June 1844 article by Thomas C Sharp, the Editor of the anti-Mormon newspaper *The Warsaw Signal*:[31]

> War and extermination is inevitable! Citizens arise, one and all!!!—Can you stand by, and suffer such infernal devils! To rob men of their property and rights, without avenging them. We have no time for comment, every man will make his own. Let it be made with powder and ball!!!

---

30   William Law, *Nauvoo Diary*, pp55-56.
31   *The Warsaw Signal* was published out of Warsaw, Illinois from 1840-1853. It took a stern stance against all things Mormon whilst favouring the Whig Party movement that was taking place in the USA at the time.

Non-Mormon followers did not favour the disregard for laws that seemed apparent regarding the attack on the *Nauvoo Expositor* and made their grievances known. On 12th June 1844, the Justice of the Peace who oversaw all events in Hancock County where the city of Nauvoo was located issued warrants for Joseph Smith and anyone else who was involved in the destruction, as it contravened freedom of speech.

It would be thirteen days before Joseph Smith and his brother Hyrum would find themselves in a jail in Carthage. Before we leave this chapter and look at what happened whilst in the jail and how they arrived there, let us not forget Jonathan Pugmire Sr, who had not long been released from jail in England for the drowning of Sarah Cartwright, and who was now in a new country with his family. They had arrived in Nauvoo only two months before the destruction of the *Nauvoo Expositor* and were unquestionably confused as to what was happening.

It is fair to say that the place they found themselves after many weeks sailing across the Atlantic was in turmoil. They had given up a life in the booming north of England to follow the words of the Prophet Joseph Smith and the teachings of the Quorum of the Twelve.

This commotion and conflict within the Mormon faith could not be helpful to the Pugmire family... could it?

# 17

# THE DEATH
# OF JOSEPH SMITH

*'I am going like a lamb to the slaughter.'*

Joseph Smith

---

It was late in the afternoon of Thursday, 27th June 1844 when Joseph Smith, the founder of Mormonism, and his older brother Hyrum Smith were attacked and killed in a hail of gunfire. An angry mob, with their faces painted black, stormed the jail at Carthage where they were being held and without warning opened fire. Joseph Smith was 38-years-old and Hyrum 44.

It seems only right that before we continue, we should go back some days prior to the attack.

After Joseph Smith had demanded the closure of the *Nauvoo Expositor* and the destruction of its premises he soon found himself in trouble with claims of his actions being a threat to the freedom of the press and unnecessary censorship. The inhabitants of Nauvoo City and indeed the wider population were not going to allow this to go without some sort of reprisal.

On 18th June 1844, aware that there would probably be repercussions, Smith declared martial law and asked for the help of the Nauvoo Legion (the State-authorised militia which numbered approximately 5,000 people). Smith wanted to be prepared when the angry, non-Mormon believers from outside of the State would come wanting retribution for his actions. He was well aware that warrants for his arrest had been issued, and a trial would be what the non-believers would demand.

This brings us to 22nd June 1844 when, after making his way

to Carthage, the Governor of Illinois, Thomas Ford,[32] suggested that a non-Mormon trial take place there. He offered this idea as he felt it would be a suitable location where Joseph Smith and other members of the Nauvoo City Council could answer fairly as to the destruction of the *Nauvoo Expositor*.

Smith, however, did not wish to wait around for such a trial. On the evening of 22nd June, along with his older brother Hyrum and several other confidentes, he crossed the famous Mississippi River in a skiff and landed in the nearby state of Iowa. They were long gone when the men sent to arrest the Smith brothers *et al* arrived.

Smith's actions in fleeing the law were criticsed by some of his followers, who subsequently questioned the authenticity of his teachings. It did not help that these followers feared for their own safety, as they found themselves threatened by troops in their homes in the city of Nauvoo.

At last showing he had a conscience, Smith deliberated and decided it would be best that he returned to Nauvoo. It is alleged that on making his decision, he said, 'If my life is of no value to my friends it is of none to myself'.[33]

Smith and his brother willingly handed themselves in at Carthage, the county seat of Illinois. It would be there that they answered the original charge of rioting and destruction. Smith would also have to answer to the charge of treason against the state of Illinois, following his declaration of martial law.

It is interesting to note that Joseph Smith was seemingly not overly concerned with the legal decision to have him arrested, and believed that it would in time be proven that he had done nothing wrong:

> I am going like a lamb to the slaughter; but I am calm as a summer's morning; I have a conscience void of offense towards God, and towards all men. I shall die innocent, and it shall yet be said of me—he was murdered in cold blood.[34]

32  5th December 1800 – 3rd November 1850 (born in Pennsylvania).
33  Church History *In The Fulness Of Times Student Manual*, (2003), 273–285.
34  Quoted in the Latter Day Saints text *Doctrine and Covenants* 135:4.

While Smith himself was confident that he was an innocent man, the non-Mormon believers did not feel the same way and reprisals followed.

# 18

# CARTHAGE CITY

*'Are you afraid to die?'*

Joseph Smith

---

In the early morning of Monday, 24th June Joseph, Hyrum and sixteen other members of the Nauvoo City Council prepped their horses and, along with a few loyal friends, climbed into their saddles, kicked their heels and rode off towards the city of Carthage.

It was at about ten o'clock when the group stopped at a farm that belonged to a man called Albert G Fellows, approximately four miles to the west of Carthage. It was here that they were met by Captain Dunn and some 60 Illinois militia men on horseback who had been waiting to accompany Joseph Smith and the others to Carthage.

Captain Dunn explained that he had an order from Governor Thomas Ford, which explained how all members of the Nauvoo Legion should relinquish their arms for fear of a resistance protesting the arrest of Joseph Smith.

Agreeing to this, Smith and the others mounted their horses and turned back the way they had come riding to Nauvoo. On their arrival Smith honoured Dunn's request and ordered that three small cannons and around 200 firearms be handed over peacefully to the militia.

At approximately six o'clock that evening Smith and the others set off once again for Carthage, eventually arriving at five minutes to midnight.

On that first night they rested at Hamilton House, where Governor Ford was also staying. The house, owned by Artois Hamilton, would be used for their hearing for the charge of inciting a riot. This was also the place where the bodies of Joseph and Hyrum Smith would be taken following the storming of the jail.

The hearing took place the next day, Tuesday 25th June, with Robert F Smith presiding. A request for bail was denied, and the brothers were incarcerated at the city jail. Among the other prisoners were Willard Richards[35] and John Taylor.[36]

After the hearing Governor Ford set off for Nauvoo. He was not the only one leaving Carthage for Nauvoo at this time; Joseph Smith sent his friend John Solomon Fullmer, who had travelled with them to Carthage, back to Nauvoo.

In actual fact Fullmer was not just a friend; he was Smith's brother-in-law. Back in July 1842, Smith's eventual successor and second president of The Church of Jesus Christ of Latter Day Saints, Brigham Young, presided over the marriage of Smith to 32-year-old Desdemona Fullmer, John Solomon's sister.

Family connections aside, Smith asked John Solomon Fullmer to find witnesses that would support him regarding the hearing of treason that was due to take place.

Fullmer agreed, and before leaving left his gun behind for the Smith brothers to protect themselves if needed. Unfortunately, on his later return back to the jail Fullmer found himself refused entry to the building and thus unable to meet once more with Joseph Smith.

Joseph spent most of Wednesday 26th June with attorneys and friends. Outside the jail people began gathering. The local anti-Mormon militia, known as the Carthage Greys, were given the task of protecting the Smith brothers and the other Nauvoo City Council members.[37]

The problem with being protected by the Greys was that they did not look favourably on Mormons or the practices they undertook. Having the actual founder of Mormonism in their very own local jail accordingly caused much despair and

---

35    24th June 1804 - 11th March 1854 (born in Massachusetts).
36    1st November 1808 – 25th July 1887 (born in Milnthorpe, Westmorland, England).
37    The actual number that made up the Carthage Greys varies dependent on the article or testimony written at the time (some reports state there were 60 men, others say there were 200).

pleasure for prisoner and protector.

Dan Jones, a Welsh-born convert to The Church of the Latter Day Saints who accompanied Smith and the others to Carthage to offer support and protection, witnessed multiple threats being made to the founder and relayed his concerns to Governor Ford. These concerns, however, were either dismissed or ignored. Ever-loyal to Joseph Smith, Dan Jones would receive one last instruction.

It was this declaration by Smith that would become known in Mormon faith as the Final Prophecy.

According to reports, Joseph Smith asked Jones, 'Are you afraid to die?'

The Welshman apparently replied to this by saying, 'Has that time come, think you? Engaged in such a cause I do not think that death would have many terrors.'

Smith replied, 'You will yet see Wales, and fulfil the mission appointed you before you die'.

Just before midnight on the 26th, the prisoners decided to position one of the wooden chairs against the door of their jail cell. They were aware that an attack could take place, and reasoned that the sound of a falling chair would hopefully wake them from their slumber.

Fortunately on that particular dark night no attack took place.

# 19

# ATTACK OF
# THE PAINTED FACES

*'I am a dead man.'*

Hyrum Smith

––––––––––––––

It was on the morning of Thursday 27th June 1844 that several pivotal things took place.

Firstly, young Welshman Dan Jones, on the advice of Joseph Smith, left Carthage for Quincy, Illinois. His journey was not without problems, however, as he found himself being shot at multiple times. Fortunately for him every bullet missed, although in his panic he ended up completely lost. He eventually arrived at Quincy late in the afternoon, whereupon he learned that it was the anti-Mormon militia with painted faces who had been shooting at him. He also discovered that Joseph and Hyrum Smith were both dead.

The second thing that took place that morning was the arrival at Carthage jail of Cyrus H Wheelock at the request of Joseph Smith. Governor Ford had approved the request, despite the fact that Wheelock's visit would not have pleased the militia guarding the prisoners. However, they were powerless to prevent the meeting.

It is interesting to know, for the arc of this story, that Cyrus Wheelock was not simply intending to exchange pleasantries with the founder of the Latter Day Saints in his hour of need; he had a definite reason for the visit, a meeting that transcended mere conversation.

––––––––––––––

John Taylor, one of the prisoners with Smith and also a member of the Quorum of the Twelve Apostles who had travelled to England in search of Mormon converts, later explained what happened on that day:

> Elder Cyrus H. Wheelock came in to see us, and when he was about leaving drew a small pistol, a six-shooter, from his pocket, remarking at the same time 'Would any of you like to have this?' Brother Joseph immediately replied, 'Yes, give it to me,' whereupon he took the pistol, and put it in his pantaloons pocket. The pistol was a six-shooting revolver, of Allen's patent; it belonged to me, and was one that I furnished to Brother Wheelock when he talked of going with me to the east, previous to our coming to Carthage.[38]

Smith still had the unshakeable belief that he would be protected and the Nauvoo Legion would come to his aid. His confidence was based on a message requesting help that he had sent to fellow Mormon Jonathan Dunham, who was the Major General of the Legion.

Dunham did receive the message, but decided not to dispatch a unit to Carthage. Governor Ford had already demanded the Nauvoo Legion be disbanded, and Dunham seemed all too aware that any action on his part could result in a civil war.

No-one was coming to the aid of the prisoners.

———————

It was late in the afternoon when the mob gathered outside the jail started to move forward and make their approach.

One of the guards, on seeing the advancing mass of people, panicked. He could see that they had used wet gunpowder to blacken their faces and this made them all the more frightening. He took a moment to think what to do, and realising what was about to happen took it upon himself to warn Joseph Smith it was him they were coming for. Smith was calm at this revelation, mistakenly believing that the mob was actually the Nauvoo

38  *History of the Church* 7:100 and *The Gospel Kingdom*, p.358.

Legion coming to rescue him.

---

The sound of many fists banging at the jail's door demanding to be allowed in was heard, and eventually they were successful.

The armed mob opened fire as they stormed through the building. Joseph Smith, realising he was not about to be rescued after all, attempted to hold closed the door of the upper room in which he, his brother and John Taylor were being held as the crowd forced their way into every room of the building looking for them.

As the painted faces approached the room where Smith and the others were being detained Hyrum was shot in the face by a bullet that passed straight through the door.

'I am a dead man', he managed to announce as he fell to the floor, dead.

Amidst the shock and confusion of what was happening, Joseph took the six-shooter in hand and began vigorously firing, his pistol aimed directly ahead as he approached the door.

---

John Taylor described what took place:

> 'I shall never forget the deep feeling of sympathy and regard manifested in the countenance of Brother Joseph as he drew nigh to Hyrum, and, leaning over him, exclaimed, 'Oh! my poor, dear brother Hyrum!' He, however, instantly arose, and with a firm, quick step, and a determined expression of countenance, approached the door, and pulling the six-shooter left by Brother Wheelock from his pocket, opened the door slightly, and snapped the pistol six successive times; only three of the barrels, however, were discharged. I afterwards understood that two or three were wounded by these discharges, two of whom, I am informed, died'.[39]

39   History of the Church of Jesus Christ of Latter-day Saints.

Taylor himself was shot four times and collapsed in a pool of his own blood. Reports of the incident state that one of the shots hit Taylor's pocket watch, saving his life. Perhaps divine intervention, perhaps one man's fortune or perhaps an officious timekeeper.

---

Eventually the mob pushed through the door and into the room where the prisoners were being held. Many bullets were exchanged with liberty. One prisoner, Willard Richards, escaped with a flesh wound to the ear, having carefully positioned himself behind the door that they had broken through.

Facing a hail of gunfire from the men with painted faces Joseph Smith ran with desperate conviction across the fallen bodies towards the window of the cell. Some reports state he was shot several times before he leapt or possibly fell from the window to the ground below.

According to some of the witnesses present at the jail in Carthage on that Thursday afternoon, the last words of Joseph Smith as he fell were, 'Oh Lord, my God!'

There are some who suggest Joseph Smith was dead before he hit the ground and there are those who maintain his lifeless body was shot several more times on the floor outside the jail by the angry mob with their blackened painted faces.

# 20

# OUR PROTAGONIST, MR PUGMIRE

*'The King is dead; long live the King'*

---

Amidst all the chaos that June afternoon in Carthage it is hard to say exactly what did or did not happen. Shots were fired, people fell from the second floor to the ground below, and lives were lost.

The result, for the purpose of this book, is that without question, at the age of 38, Joseph Smith Jr, the founder of Mormonism, was dead and a martyr was born.

---

The main character of this story, Jonathan Pugmire Sr, and most of his family would arrive at Salt Lake City in 1847, a year after future leader Brigham Young. Fortunately for Jonathan, his experience as a blacksmith and his apparent diplomacy proved invaluable for both him and his eldest son, Jonathan Jr, as they had a trade that they could offer to the flourishing Mormon community.

But now, Joseph Smith - the leader, founder, translator and creator of the *Book of Mormon*, and the reason why Jonathan Pugmire Sr left Liverpool - was dead.

The King is dead, long live the King... Step forward Brigham Young.

# 21

# THE SUCCESSION CRISIS

*'Letter of appointment'*

---

To understand the naming and history of Salt Lake City, Utah where the Pugmires decided to travel to it is necessary to know about the so-called 'Succession Crisis', which began almost immediately after the death of Joseph Smith, when a group of people put themselves forward as the next potential leader of the Latter Day Saint movement.

The main three people involved in the crisis and who featured in the race to become the next leader were:

## Sidney Rigdon (1793-1876)

An early friend of Joseph Smith who was tarred and feathered with him in the Ohio incident of 1832 following the negative reaction to the publication of *The Book of Mormon*. Rigdon was also a member of the First Presidency[40] and was seen as the next leader.

## Brigham Young (1801-1877)

A convert to Mormonism after reading *The Book of Mormon*, and eventual leader of the early Mormon movement in the north of England. The ever-powerful Young dismissed the claim of Strang, and disputed Rigdon's right to take over from Joseph Smith.

---

40   Members of the First Presidency are chosen to oversee and instruct in all things to do with the Latter Day Saints.

## James J Strang (1813-1856)

A relatively new convert into the Church of the Latter Day Saints,[41] Strang staked a claim to lead the movement as he had what is known as the Letter of Appointment. The letter in question was suggested as being written by Joseph Smith just a week before he was shot and killed at the jail in Carthage. Those who supported Strang believed the letter to show that he was specifically chosen as the next to lead the movement. The question of the authenticity of the letter however has continued to be debated ever since it first appeared in 1844.

---

Despite the other voices of those claiming to be the rightful successor, Brigham Young maintained that as a chosen member of the Quorum of the Twelve Apostles[42] he had power over them all, despite the fact that fellow candidate Sidney Rigdon had served as an original counsellor of the First Presidency.

So it was that following many meetings, conferences, gatherings and garnering of popular support, it was Brigham Young who became the successor to Joseph Smith. This was cemented when he was voted leader at a conference that took place on 8th August 1844 in Nauvoo, Illinois.

Sidney Rigdon and James Strang would not accept the decision, however, and individually continued with their own branch of Mormonism.

---

The internal power struggle for leadership would not concern Jonathan Pugmire Sr at this point. He had just arrived from England and his main concern was looking after his family as they found themselves in a new country.

---

41  Baptized on 25th February 1844 by Joseph Smith.
42  Representatives of Mormonism who travel to meet and preach to people who are not members of the Latter Day Saints.

# 22

# THE NAMING OF SALT LAKE CITY

## *'Who was Brigham Young?'*

So it was that on 24th July 1847[43] Brigham Young, the second President of the Latter Day Saints, travelled to the Salt Lake Valley in Utah. On arrival he looked across the rocks and the arid dry land and proclaimed the new city Salt Lake City.

Before continuing with what happened after the naming of Salt Lake City, let us go back and I will tell you about the man called Brigham Young. He has been mentioned multiple times in the course of this story and will be mentioned often as this book continues. As I have explained, he was chosen as a missionary by Joseph Smith himself and sent on a missionary role overseas. It would be wrong not to mention again that he became the head of the overseas Mormon Church that was based in Preston in the north of England, something Jonathan Pugmire Sr would have been excited by.

So who exactly was the newly-appointed successor to Joseph Smith and new President of the Latter Day Saints?

Brigham Young was born on 1st of June 1801 in Whitingham, Vermont to parents John Young and Abigail Howe. Young plied his trade as a blacksmith and carpenter. In 1824, as a newly-practising Methodist, Young married his first wife, a woman called Miriam Angeline Works.

---

43   This is known as Pioneer Day in Utah.

In 1830 he discovered the newly published *The Book of Mormon*,[44] and in 1835 became a member of the first Quorum of the Twelve Apostles, the group of people sent overseas to preach the word of Mormon and Joseph Smith.

In 1844, following the death of Joseph Smith, there was a Succession Crisis, resulting in several people, including Young, vying for the position of head of the Church of Jesus Christ of Latter Day Saints. As you have read, Brigham Young became the next leader.

On 24th July 1847, along with his fellow Mormon followers, Young arrived at the Salt Lake Valley in Utah to begin a new life. In December of that year he was ordained President of the Church.

In 1876 Young ordained our main character, an elderly Jonathan Pugmire Sr, as Patriarch.

---

44　The book was first published on 26th March 1830 in Palmyra, New York.

# 23

# THE PUGMIRE TRAVELS

*'We moved across the river to*
*Montrose, Lee County, Iowa'*

Joseph Hyrum Pugmire

---

Returning back to the June of 1844, following the death of Joseph Smith and his brother Hyrum not everything was going as hoped for the Pugmire family. In fact, poor Elizabeth Pugmire, Jonathan's wife, was far from happy.

The Pugmire family had only been at Nauvoo for a few weeks and Elizabeth was feeling anxious and more than a little uncomfortable after learning what had happened to Joseph Smith and the others with him. She was worried about the possible repercussions in the city where they found themselves over the attacking of Mormon followers, and so it was not long before the Pugmire family decided to leave Nauvoo and move on.

For a rural family from the north of England, such events would undoubtedly be traumatic. They had, after all, sacrificed everything to make the journey to the United States and within a few weeks the prophet, founder and leader of the religion they had joined had been murdered.

---

By the April of 1846 the Pugmire family would find themselves in Montrose, Lee County, Iowa, where Elizabeth would give birth to a son they called Moroni. Unfortunately, records show that he lived for just one day.

One son of Jonathan and Elizabeth, Joseph Hyrum Pugmire,

who was 10-years-old when they left England, wrote of this period in his latter years:

> My mother, being a very nervous person, she could not stand the troubles in Nauvoo after the Prophet and his brother Hyrum were murdered, so we moved across the river to Montrose, Lee County, Iowa.

It is clear that the move from England to America did not afford Elizabeth Pugmire immediate comfort. The struggles encountered at this time were highlighted in the reflections of Joseph Hyrum:

> While living in Montrose, my father and my brother Jonathan Jr. were called to help prepare wagons for those going westward to find a home for the Saints. After staying in this area for some 5 months my father Jonathan Pugmire Sr. was called by John Taylor[45] to go to Winter Quarters[46] to work at his trade of blacksmithing outfitting wagons for the trip of the Saints across the Plains. Enroute from Montrose, Iowa to Winter Quarters we traveled in Captain Danses' Company.

It would be three long years after arriving in the state of Illinois before the Pugmire family reached the Salt Lake Valley and the city that what would became known as Salt Lake City.

---

45  See Chapter 4.
46  The Church of the Latter Day Saints encampment in Nebraska.

# 24

# THE WINTER QUARTERS

*'These with scurvy made me helpless indeed!'*

Louisa Barnes Pratt

———————

So we now find the Pugmire family living in the state of Iowa. This would not last for long though, and after gathering together the belongings which they had brought with them from England, they set off on their travels once more. The next stop for the Pugmires would be a Mormon encampment known as the Winter Quarters. This was a place of safety set up in North Omaha, Nebraska and the location for the Mormon headquarters whilst the new converts saw out the long winter before continuing on their journey west across the United States.

The Winter Quarters, which was always supposed to be only a temporary camp, would prove to be a disaster for many of the newly-converted Mormon families involved in the migration. Scurvy (which they called blackleg) was common due to the diet of bread, bacon and milk and a lack of vegetables. The encampment also had to deal with the devastating effects of tuberculosis and malaria.

———————

Unfortunately, it was while at the Winter Quarters that on 3rd November 1846 Elizabeth Pugmire died. The cold and harsh conditions were too much for her. This must have been hard for Jonathan, as they had been together ever since they married at Carlisle, Cumberland some 25 years earlier, when Jonathan was 21 and Elizabeth not yet 20.

Elizabeth was not the only to succumb here, however, as

many other people died due to the poor diet and disease. Louisa Barnes Pratt,[47] a Mormon missionary who would later challenge for the right of women to vote, was also in the Winter Quarters at this time. A keen writer of her experiences, Louisa wrote of this difficult time in Nebraska:

> I hired a man to build me a sod cave. He took turf from the earth, laid it up, covered it with willow brush and sods. Built a chimney of the same... I paid a five dollar gold piece for building my sod house, 10 x 12... A long cold rain storm brought more severely again the chills and fever. These with scurvy made me helpless indeed!... Many of my friends sickened and died in that place, when I was not able to leave my room, could not go to their bedside to administer comfort to them in the last trying hours, not even to bid them farewell. Neither could I go to see their remains carried to their final resting place where it was thought I would shortly have to be conveyed.[48]

Eventually the winter did subside, and with the approach of spring the Mormon faithful packed up their wagons and continued on their journey to the west, next stop Utah.

------

47   1802-1880.
48   *History of Louisa Barnes Pratt*, Utah State University Press 1998.

# 25

# MOVING TO CEDAR CITY, IRON COUNTY, UTAH

*'I stopped in the street opposite
Pugmire & Cartwright's black-smith's shop for repairs'*

Thomas Dunlop Brown

---

As described earlier, not everything went to plan for the Pugmires as they travelled across the United States. The death of Elizabeth was a great loss to both Jonathan and their children.

Finding themselves separated from their father, the Pugmire children left the Winter Quarters and travelled the last leg with the John Taylor Company that was made up of approximately 70 wagons and 200 people.

The Horne fifty (also known as the John Taylor company) consisted of 72 wagons and 197 people. The captains of tens were Ariah C. Brower, Abraham Hoagland, Archibald Gardner, William Taylor, and Thomas Orr Sr. Included in the first ten led by Ariah C. Brower were: Elizabeth Boyes, Samuel Bringhurst, Ann Elizabeth Brower, Ariah Coates Brower, Ariah Hussey Brower, Margaret E. Hussey Brower, Victoria Adelide Brower, Ann Cannon, George Q. Cannon, William Farrar, Elizabeth Cole Holmes, Robert Holmes, Elizabeth Ann Horne, Henry James Horne, Joseph Horne, Joseph Smith Horne, Mary Isabelle Horne, Richard Stephen Horne, Ann Kelly, John Mackay, James I. Orr, Elizabeth Pugmire, Hannah Pugmire, John Pugmire, Jonathan Pugmire, Joseph Hyrum Pugmire, Mary Pugmire, Helenora Symonds, William Symonds, Annie B. Taylor, Elizabeth K. Taylor, George J. Taylor, Jane Ballantyne Taylor, John

Taylor, Joseph Taylor, Leonora Cannon Taylor, Mary Ann Taylor, Mary Ann Taylor, Sophia Whittaker Taylor, Maria L. Woodward, and Alexander Wright.[49]

---

Finally, on 25th September 1847, almost a year after the death of his wife, Jonathan Pugmire Sr and his children reached their initial destination. They had made it and arrived at the Great Salt Lake Valley, Utah.

What follows is a record of the pioneer travels to Salt Lake in Utah in 1847.

'The company that arrived in the Great Salt Lake Valley in late September 1847 consisted of these hundreds:

1st hundred (Darrell Spencer) arrived Sep 24, 1847

2nd hundred (Edward Hunter) arrived Sep 29, 1847

3rd hundred (Jedidia Grant) arrived Oct 2, 1847

4th hundred (Abraham Smoot) arrived Sept 25, 1847

Charles C Rich's Guard arrived Oct 2, 1847

From the 2nd hundred of Cpt Edward Hunter, its 50, captained by Joseph Horne and its 1st 10 by Ariel C. Brower. Of some 30 members were the following:

John Taylor

George Q Cannon

Jonathan Pugmire, b. 28 Mar 1799, Welton, Cumberland, England

Mary

Hyrum Joseph (Joseph Hyrum)

Elizabeth

John

Hannah

The pioneers traveled generally together, with various hundreds reversing their order from time to time. It was sort of a game of catch-up as the road was more or less passable.

---

49   Taken from the research of Pugmire family descendents.

Several individual diaries give us the tenor of the trip. Patty Sessions, Charles Rich, Howard Egan and various clerks of the 100's and 50's all kept diaries. The diaries tell of passing burned out indian villages and of living in dreaded fear of indian sightings, often seeing them creep up to the camp both day and night. Many little children were run over by wagons, but most survived after administrations. The wagons weighed up to 3500 pounds. The pioneers went from feast to famine, sometimes they thirsted terrible for want of water and other times the wagons were severely beaten by torrential rains. Hell, fire and brimstone were commonplace in their religious services, for, example, for stealing, they were told that their posterity would be stained throughout all eternity. After two weeks out, them came upon traves of their previous brethren, a board marked "Camp of Pioneers" and dated Apr 29th. What joy and determination filled their souls.

The following excerpt probably portrays much of their journey:

hunters returned with 4 buffalo, 2 deer and 1 antelope

200 Pawnees were sighted. They do not want us traveling through their lands.

The morning was dull and warm'.[50]

---

It did not take long for Jonathan to set to work helping in the development of the newly colonised city:

The first settlers in the ward were persons who built homes there in the fall of 1848 instead of residing in the Old Fort, Jonathan Pugmire, Sr., built the first real house in the area, and other early residents were George Whitaker, Thomas H. Woodbury and Charles Lambert.[51]

The Salt Lake City maps of this time show the Pugmire family

50    *The Pioneers of 1847* book US/CAN 929.2 W2p film Europe 1183516 item 10.
51    'Pioneers and Prominent Men of Utah', (Frank Esshom) 1913.

living on the corner of Third South and West Temple, Block 50, Lot 5. Recalling their time there, Joseph Pugmire explained how they 'lived on roots for the first six months and continued to be hungry for two or three years.'

There would be other plans for Jonathan Pugmire Sr, however, and his stay in the newly-created Salt Lake City would not last long.

---

It was in 1850 that Jonathan Pugmire Sr found himself chosen as part of the Iron Mission, a project instigated by Brigham Young with the sole purpose of mining Utah for as much iron as possible. As a member of the Iron Mission, Jonathan Pugmire Sr and his family left their home in Salt Lake City and moved to Cedar City, Utah in the newly-created county known as Iron County.

Cedar City, which was the largest city in Iron County, is situated approximately 250 miles south of Salt Lake City and it would be where Jonathan and his family would call home for the next eight years. It was at Cedar City that he and his good friend from the days back in Cheshire, Thomas Cartwright, opened up their very own blacksmiths shop.

---

The early days in Iron County were described in the biography of Henry Lunt, a Mormon missionary who left his home in Cheshire, England for America, which was collated by author Evelyn K Jones. The biography contained a specific mention of Jonathan's friend Thomas Cartwright in an 1851 journal entry by Lunt:

> On Friday, January 31, the camp was called together... all was reported well in camp save one man, brother Thomas Cartwright, who unluckily cut one of his middle toes off with his axe.

Journals were a popular pastime it would seem, as a fellow

convert to Mormonism who came from Scotland and had also crossed the Atlantic to join with the other followers kept a record of his exploits. His name was Thomas Dunlop Brown, and he on 18th July 1854 wrote about his own arrival at Cedar City, Utah:

> Started back early for and arrived at Cedar City and as one of my tires had come off on the road I stopped in the street opposite Pugmire & Cartwright's black-smith's shop for repairs.[52]

---

52  *Journal of the Southern Indian Mission*, published in 1972 by the Utah State University Press.

# 26

# YOUNG JOHN PUGMIRE

*'It was supposed to have been accidentally done'*

Henry Lunt

---

Relocation to Cedar City, Utah was not without tragedy for Jonathan Pugmire Sr.

In 1852, whilst out herding cattle in the city of Parowan, near Cedar City, his son John Pugmire was shot and killed. He was not yet twelve-years-old when the stray bullet ended his young life.

Henry Lunt kept extensive journals of his experiences and this also included details on the shooting of John Pugmire, which in turn appeared in the biography by Evelyn K. Jones:

> While herding cattle, Brother Robert Owen's son, Jerome, shot Brother Pugmire's son on January 2, 1852. Henry Lunt stated, 'It was supposed to have been accidentally done'. John D Lee wrote, 'It was a shocking occurrence. Whether the boy was shot designedly or not was a consideration that remained to be proved'. Young Owen was tried, or rather examined, before Lee and Squire Leyno and held to bail for his appearance at the next term of the District Court. Circumstantial evidence was strong against him.

What happened would have clearly devastated Jonathan and his surviving family. This would be the fifth child to have died following sons Joseph, Richard, William and Moroni, on top of his involvement in the drowning of his friend's wife in Cheshire in 1843, and the death of his wife Elizabeth in 1846 in Nebraska. Jonathan Pugmire Sr would carry on forward though, and focus on the blacksmith shop he had opened at Cedar City with his friend Thomas Cartwright.

By the first part of 1853 decisions were made to reshape the ironworks at Cedar City. The Deseret Iron Company was created. Among many of the shareholders in the company was Thomas Cartwright.

The 1857 Iron County Militia Project explained:

> 'As they refined the design of their blast furnace, Cartwright used his skills to make tuyeres and other specialized equipment for the complicated blasting process. During this time, while most men worked an average of thirty days on the furnace, iron specialists such as Cartwright, Thomas Bladen, and Jonathan Pugmire each worked more than one hundred days.

---

In the summer of 1853 a war took place that is known as the Walker War. This particular confrontation led to people such as Pugmire and Cartwright stopping work at the furnace and focussing on strengthening the wall around where they living in Cedar City. Progress was slow, however, and by Christmas of 1853 the then Bishop, Philip Klingensmith, told the Mormon pioneers that there would be no dance organised over the festive period until the wall was finished.

According to the 1857 Iron County Militia Project,

> 'the young people felt otherwise and convinced Cartwright, the community fiddler, to play for them. When the dance was underway, Bishop Klingensmith found the holiday revelers, closed the dance, and "cut off" all those, including Cartwright, who had violated his edict. Cartwright appealed Klingensmith's precipitous decision to the high council. Finally, cooler heads prevailed and Cartwright and the others was restored to full fellowship in the church and community'.

---

# 27

# THE DIARY OF THOMAS DUNLOP BROWN

*'By the kindness of Jonathan Pugmire Senr.*
*I had a room in his new house'*

Thomas Dunlop Brown

---

One man who kept a diary of his experiences as a Mormon in mid-19th century America was the man from Scotland previously mentioned, Thomas Dunlop Brown who, like Jonathan Pugmire Sr, had baptized into the Church of the Latter Day Saints back in Liverpool some years before, in the 1840s.

What makes the diary of Dunlop Brown important to this story is that Jonathan Pugmire Sr is mentioned in it on numerous occasions.

---

So who was Thomas Dunlop Brown?

He was born in Stewarton, Ayrshire on 16th December 1807 to father James Galt Brown, a weaver, and mother Agnes Johnston Dunlop. He married Sarah Godwin and together they started a family which included a son named James Godwin Brown (1842-1886) and a daughter, Sarah Godwin Brown (1843).

Prior to converting, Thomas was a teacher in various schools. It was whilst teaching in Lancashire that he first became aware of Mormonism and it would not be long after his awakening that he was baptized into the faith. The date of his baptism - and the moment he became a member of the Church of the Latter Day Saints - was 9th June 1844, and it took place in Liverpool.

It was some years later, in 1852, that Thomas boarded a ship, crossed the Atlantic and made his way to the Salt Lake Valley. He was not alone, however, as he took his family with him where they could start a new life and devote themselves to the Church of the Latter Day Saints.

This brings us to the diary. It was from 10th April 1854 to 10th January 1857 that Thomas kept a detailed account of everything that happened, and excitingly within these handwritten pages are some several references to Jonathan Pugmire Sr.

The following excerpts are taken directly from the written records of Thomas Dunlop Brown, which were published for all to read in 1972 by the Utah State University Press. The collection was given the title *Journal of the Southern Indian Mission*, and all words are his own.

----

## JOURNAL OF THE SOUTHERN INDIAN MISSION
### by Thomas Dunlop Brown

### Saturday 20th May 1854.

> Saw Brors Thomas Cartwright, Jonathan Pugmire, Geo. Johnson, Geo. Wood and spent an evening of intelligence.

As can be seen from this entry, Thomas Cartwright and Jonathan Pugmire Sr have remained friends following what happened in Crewe back in 1843, and are both now in Utah.

Tuesday 18th July 1854.

> Started back early for and arrived at Cedar City and as one of my tires had come off on the road I stopped in the street opposite Pugmire & Cartwright's black-smith's shop for repairs, ( & here I remained during hay harvesting season till I went home to Conference following September ) ate with Brors Liston & Bosnell, and truly I was glad once more to sit down to a good meal with white men; Brors Allen, Atwood, Knights, Burges and Haskell went to Parowan to work - Brors. Brown, Hatch, Dickson, Thornton, Robinson

& Knell stayed to work for bread in Cedar City. Bror Allen returned to Cedar City, & Bror Dickson commenced teaching there.

This entry shows that both Jonathan and Thomas made use of the experience they had as blacksmiths back in England and had opened up their own shop together.

## Monday 24th July 1854.

Awoke in Cedar City by the firing of Carmon,&c. under care of Capt. R. Keys. Spent this day with Prest. Pugmire, who with the High Council were escorted to the Tabernacle by the citizens & the military under Cap. Key & City Marshal C. P. Liston. The day was too hot to walk around the fort 2 miles. We walked from the President's house up the east line, out at the gate towards the Iron Works turning at Snow & Bosnell's mill: I was appointed Orator of the day, in the absence of I .C. Haight who had gone to G.S.L. City.

This entry shows that Jonathan Pugmire Sr was not just a follower of Mormonism, he was held in some esteem by the others within the community and had a position that was respected.

## Wednesday 2nd to Saturday 5th August 1854.

Missionaries have no home but their wagons, by the kindness of Jonathan Pugmire Senr. I had a room in his new house part finished.

Whilst Jonathan may have accidentally drowned his friend's wife back in England, this entry shows his compassionate side and a desire to help.

## Sunday 6th August 1854.

Prest. Pugmire spoke on the second coming of Christ followed by T.D. Brown on the extent of Salvation to the dead as well as to the living. Dined with Jehiel McConnell, afternoon a general testimony meeting.

Again this entry shows the position of Pugmire within the community. It is also interesting to note that Thomas Dunlop Brown referred to himself in the third person when writing down the day's events.

### Sunday 20th August 1854.

At meeting. J. Pugmire, Senr. sick, Joel H. Johnson presided.

### Monday 28th August 1854.

Attended a meeting this evening to arrange a discussion between R. Dickson & Arthur Parker on English Crammer." Question Whether the Old System of English Grammar, or Brown's new system of Syntithology is the better. James Lewis of Parowan & T.D. Brown were appointed to judge & decide: Jnon. Pugmire Chairman: Brors Bosnell, Harrison & Liston Committee.

Again we can see that at this meeting Pugmire was elected Chairman, and so must have had quite a standing amongst his peers.

### Friday 27th October 1854.

Arrived in Cedar City here we were detained to Sunday 5 Nov. for repairs of my waggon wheels. J. Pugmire Senr. was very kind to me and mine & during our stay J. Sherratt & D. Tullis dug potatoes for him & Geo. Wood; & on.

Thomas was clearly very thankful for the support given to him by Jonathan Pugmire.

### Wednesday 27th December 1854.

In Deseret Iron Coy's store assisting C. Arthur. Missionaries boys returned home, the following have been kind to us strangers, Brors. Pugmire, Bosnel, Walker, McMurdie, P. Fife, R. Wylie & others they have fed & lodged us.

## Sunday 7th January 1855.

Sharp shooting in the meeting between Brors Haight, Pugmire & the Bishop P.K. Smith about the Still. The latter opposed to it.

This entry is very interesting as it mentions Bishop P K Smith and a meeting that was held between him, Pugmire and Isaac C Haight. There will be further interaction between P K Smith and Jonathan later.

## Tuesday 16th January 1855.

Very cold frosty night. During all this cold weather, I slept in Jno. Pugmire's new house- very open -a Buffalo robe only under me, same & top coat over me - a bag of clothes for my pillow. Such is life in a new frontier wilderness country. They had plenty of good coal & a grateful, after the English fashion was always kindled when I lay down - if possible to warm the air a little. Thawed during the day.

Thomas Dunlop Brown was obviously very grateful for the hospitality shown by Pugmire.

## Thursday 25th January 1855.

Jno Stoddard had Kershaw given him to wife this day by Jno. Pugmire Senr., 1 was present. The first Iron this day from Trial Furnace of Iron Coy. was slightly rolled & squeezed on Pugmire's hearth, instead of being puddle it was wrought into a slightly malleable Iron rod, part of it sent to President Young & some nails made out of the balance. I have 2 in my purse made by Pugmire Senr.

Again, we can see from this entry the role Pugmire played in the Cedar City community.

## Sunday 28th January 1855.

> Prest. Pugmire cleaned the Tabernacle at Cedar City after plastering.

Jonathan Pugmire Sr was happy to get involved with the community and chores that may have been seen as unimportant by some.

## Tuesday 13th February 1855.

> Returned from Parowan on foot with W.W. Willis, left my dog and gun Barrel with Wm. Mitchell Junr. To bring on. Bishop P.K. Smith and Prest. Jnon. Pugmire locking horns.

They were indeed locking horns, as allegations against Bishop P K Smith had been raised regarding his treatment of his wife and it was Jonathan Pugmire Sr who was sought after to deal with the matter.

## Thursday 15th February 1855.

> All day in Jonathan Pugmire's, hearing the recital by Sister P.K. Smith of her husbands abuse, at Nauvoo, Sanpete & here. She was applying for council from I.C. Haight & Jnon. Pugmire.

The details of this day will be discussed later on.

## Friday 16th February 1855.

> In Iron Coy's office, finishing my engagement in C. Arthur's place, wages allowed $2.50 per day, or 50¢ more than their Common laborers! they allow mechanics $3.00 & masons $4.00 per day. A Book-keeper's experience & intelligence of less value here, than the bone and sinew. C. Arthur offered voluntarily to make up out of his salary a sufficient amount to remunerate m~ for my services. I paid Jnon. Pugmire for my board. He was liberal with me, as also were Jos. Walker's family, Jas Bosnel's, Jehiel McConnel's &c. They

did my washing &c. free. So also were P. M. Fife's family & Jno. Hamilton's, ministering to my necessities.

## Monday 19th February 1855.

A private meeting of the High Council in Prest. Pugmire's on P.K. Smith's Family affairs. At 9 o'clock, moon 3rd day old, and till next morning only about 2 inches fell.

The reason for this private gathering will be explained later. For the moment, it is important to remember that P K Smith was a respected Bishop within the Mormon faith. On this particular day, Jonathan Pugmire Sr had been asked to chair the meeting and come to a decision on what may have happened regarding the family affairs of Bishop P K Smith.

———————————

The diary of Thomas Dunlop Brown offers a valuable insight into not only life as part of the arriving Mormons at Utah, but also Jonathan Pugmire Sr's importance within the community in Utah.

The entries also show that Pugmire and Thomas Cartwright remained friends after the unfortunate incident that took place in the river in Crewe, the subsequent prison stay and trial. In fact, not only did they remain friends but they both relocated to Cedar City and opened up a blacksmith's shop together.

As for Thomas Dunlop Brown, he married again to a woman called Mary Lucretia Willis (1837-1912). Together they had children John William, Emily and Francis Elonzo Brown. Thomas died on 20th March 1874 in Salt Lake City.

———————————

# 28

# THE RECITAL OF
# SISTER P K SMITH

*'All day in Jonathan Pugmire's, hearing the recital*
*by Sister P.K. Smith of her husband's abuse'*

Thomas Dunlop Brown

---

The diary of Thomas Dunlop Brown shows how Jonathan Pugmire Sr involved himself in the physical aspects of setting up a new community. How would he fare when faced with a problem that was more of a personal manner?

You are about to find out.

---

On 15th February 1855 a somewhat distressed woman appeared at the front door of Pugmire's house in Cedar City, Utah. The woman in question was called Hannah, and she was married to Philip Klingon Smith (also known as Klingensmith), a respected and powerful bishop within the Latter Day Saints.

In a session between Hannah and Jonathan that lasted the whole day, she explained how she was suffering from domestic violence and felt she could not live with it anymore. This was quite the event, as Klingon Smith was an important man and a wife that speaks out against the treatment of women in 19th century America by their spouse under the umbrella of Mormon faith is a brave person.

---

Who were Hannah and Philip Klingon Smith?

Hannah, whose full name was Hannah Henry Creamer, was born in the state of Ohio on 14th April 1826 and died on 10th March 1891 in Panaca, Nevada. Philip was born in Brush Creek, Westmoreland in the state of Pennsylvania in 1825 and is thought to have died around 1881, possibly in Mexico. They were married on 28th February 1841.

Hannah was one of three women who had been married to Klingon Smith. It would take some time for her to leave her husband. Turning up to the house of Jonathan Pugmire Sr shows the distress she was in. She would be finally divorced from her husband in 1871.

As for Philip Klingon Smith, eventually he would be excommunicated from the Mormon Church following the events that took place at the Mountain Meadows in 1857, something that is soon to be discussed.

# 29

# CEDAR CITY WARD RELIEF SOCIETY

*'Sister Pugmire and sister [Alice] Randle said that
the sisters manifested a good spirit and seemed to
be improving, that they encouraged them to live
their religion, and to continue to improve.'*

Ellen Lunt

---

It was at Cedar City, Utah where Jonathan Pugmire Sr married
his third wife. Her name was Elizabeth South. Born on 9th May
1802 in England, she was a cousin of his second wife Mary.
They were married in 1856, and would remain together for the
next 20 years.

---

As tensions rose between the Mormon settlers in Utah and
those from other states who were opposed to their way of life,
the women at Cedar City came up with a way in which they
could help support the men.

It was on 20th November 1856 that Isaac C Haight gathered
together almost all of the women who were living at Cedar City.
It was on this day in the local tabernacle that the Cedar City
Ward Relief Society was formed.

---

A woman named Lydia Hopkins was voted President, and
chose Annabella Sinclair MacFarlane Haight, wife of Isaac C
Haight, as her first Counsellor. Lancashire-born Ellen Whittaker

Lunt was chosen to take the minutes, transcripts of which follow. The ladies generally met together one Thursday afternoon a month. Unfortunately, due to the lack of good quality iron at Cedar City, and the massacre that would take place at Mountain Meadows in the September of 1857, the Society in its original form did not last for long.

What follows are the minutes of three meetings as taken down by Ellen Lunt between September 1857 and March 1858. The minutes were written down on different sizes of paper, as the women who came to the meeting donated spare pieces of paper for her to record the events on.

The first record was taken one day before the tragedy at Mountain Meadows, which will be discussed next.

---

### Thursday 10th September 1857.

Met according to appointment 2, o, clock p.m. Thursday Sep<u>r</u> 10<u>th</u> 1857. Opened the meeting by singing, Prayer by Sister Lunt, Singing <Minutes read and approved> Sister Hopkins called for the teachers report Sister Pugmire and sister [Alice] Randle said that the sisters manifested a good spirit and seemed to be improving, that they encouraged them to live their religion, and to continue to improve. Sister Liston said that she with sister [Mary] Mc Connell had visited the north line, and that they ~~they~~ found the sisters doing pretty well, that they instructed them in cleanliness economy &c. felt highly pleased with the sisters as a general thing Sister Willis and Sister Haight said that they found things generally to their satisfaction taught them the necessity of being obedient to their husbands &c— and not to be fearful in these troublesome times but to be prayerful and attend to their duties. Mother Whittaker and Sister Annabella found the sisters generally enjoying a good spirit, that they felt to rejoice in visiting the sisters & that they felt the sisters were improveing in all things Sister Haight said that the sisters enjoyed a better spirit than they did eight or nine months ago,— said that these were squally times, and we ought to attend to secret prayer in behalf of our husbands, sons, fathers, & brothers. instructed the sisters to teach their sons & daughters the principles of righteousness, and to implant a desire in their hearts to avenge the blood of the Prophets

Sister Hopkins said that she with sister White had visited the sisters in the middle lines, that they felt well and manifested a good spirit, and was desirous to do well, and to improve,— advised them to attend strictly to secret prayer in behalf of the brethren that are out acting in our defence.—The Presidency gave some good instructions to the sisters, which if adhered to, would tend greatly to their benefit.— Sister Liston & Sister Mc-Connell were appointed to visit the East line. Sister Pugmire and Sister Randle the Middle lines, Sister [Mary Ann] Harrison and Sister White the South line. Sister Mc-Murdy [Mary Ann McMurdie] <& Sister [Barbara] Morris> the West line. The Presidency would take the North line. Sister Eliza Ann Haight & Sister Willis the Iron works & the new City.— Sung—Oh how glorious will be the morning &c.— Sister [Celestia] Durfee, Sister Wilden, Mother [Barbara] Morris, Sister [Terressa] Chamberlain, Sister Randle & Sister Jane Bosnell bore their [p. [18]] testimony and felt to rejoice that the time of our redemption was drawing nigh. It was moved and carried, that Margaret Bateman Hannah K Smith [Klingensmith], Hannah Micholston [Ane Mickelsen] become members of this Society. Sister Hopkins said the bell would be rung half an hour before meeting time for the future. Singing. Benediction by Sister Mary Willis. Adjourned till 2 o clock p.m. Thursday Octr 8th 1857. Ellen Lunt—Secretary... [p. [19]]...

## Thursday 10th December 1857.

Met Pursuant to adjournment 2 o clock p.m. Thursday Dec 10th 1857. Present, Bishop Smith [Phillip Klingensmith], & Elder Henry Lunt. Opened the meeting by Singing Prayer by the Bishop. Singing. Minutes read & accepted. Sister Haight called for a report from the teachers. Sister Pugmire & Sister Randle reported the Sisters on the South line as enjoying a good spirit and doing the best they could. they didn't feel to find any fault with them but felt well with improvement some of them had made, Sister White and Sister Mary-Ann Harrison spent a pleasant day in visiting the sisters on the West line, who were enjoying a good spirit and felt content with their lot, and desirous to live their religion. Sister Liston said, through circumstances unavoidable they didn't visit the Sisters this month, but she felt desirous to do right & to do her duty in all things. Sister Morris said they found the sisters on the north line, doing well and enjoying a good spirit. Sister Eliza Ann Haight said that like Sister Liston they had been prevented from visiting the sisters through circumstances &c. Mother Whittaker & Sister Annabella found the sisters on the East line glad to see them they were enjoying a good spirit but like the rest of the sisters on the other lines as the teachers had reported, were destitute of clothing, they advised the Sisters who had plenty, to cultivate a liberal spirit and administer to the poor, also for those who didn't know how to learn and manufacture their own clothing. Bishop Smith then said, it was some time since he was here before but he thought he would come to day said he was well pleased with this Society and the reports given, and that the sisters felt about right. Spoke on being destitute of clothing, said that it was quite right, and that it was good for us, but there was always a way opened when it was most needed.— Spoke considerable on home manufacture etc. Bro Lunt then arose, and made some very appropriate remarks, spoke on cleanliness, and a many other principles of the Kingdom and said that the sisters would do well to adhere unto the counsel given by the Bishop.— Sister A Haight felt to rejoice in what the brethren had said & exhorted the sisters to listen to the teachings and act thereupon. appointed the teachers to visit the same lines this month as they did the last. but if it was bad weather they needn't go round and it was expected the sisters would do their duty whether the teachers went round or not [p. [21]] It was moved and seconded that Mary-Ann Lunt, Agnes Easton[,] Catherine Whittaker, & Louisa Hunt become members of this Society, carried unanimously. The Bishop again arose, and acquiesced in what Sister Haight had said and encouraged the Sisters to go on in the good work Sister Randle spoke on the wants of the treasury. closed the meeting by singing Benediction by Elder Lunt. Adjourned till 2 o clock p.m. Thursday January 14th 1858

Ellen Lunt—Secretary... [p. [22]]...

## Thursday 11th March 1858.

Met again at the appointed time & place, 2. o. clock p.m. Thursday, March 11th 1858. <Sister Hopkins, Presided.> Opened the meeting by singing. Prayer by Sister Ann White. Singing.— [p. [24]] The president called for the teachers report. Sister Pugmire and sister Randle reported the Sisters on the west line feeling well, and manifested a good spirit, and were trying to do the best they could. Sister Harrison & Sister Lund found the sisters on the north line endeavouring to live their religion and most of their habitations were nice and clean. Sister Morris reported the sisters in the middle lines, doing well, with few exceptions, had no fault to find with them. Sister White and sister Mc-Connell found the sisters on the East line enjoying a good spirit, and they believed the sisters were improving Sister Haight & Sister Willis found the sisters in the new City enjoying the good spirit of the Lord, but she didn't find them so well supplied in clothing. Sister Hopkins with sister A Haight & Mother Whittaker enjoyed their visit to the sisters on the south line very much. found them enjoying a good spirit generally, and trying to live their religion. counselled the mothers to instruct their children in every good thing. Sister Haight said she would like for those who understood home manufacture to teach those that didn't. Spoke on bringing some patches to the treasury that there might be some covers made for the benefit of the poor that she wouldn't like to be a whit behind any other society in the mountains. Spoke considerable for the benefit of the sisters. Mother Whittaker said it was rejoicing to her to see the progress the sisters were making in this Society. counselled the sisters to be cautious how they spoke one of another. The President then gave the sisters the privilege to speak their minds. Sister [Roxsena] Patten said she wished to be one with us and whilst sitting down she had been reflecting on the scenes she had witnessed in Nauvoo. Said that she had long been deprived of the privilege that we now enjoyed. Sung Come Come ye Saints &c.— Sister Annabella said that if any of the sisters thought of any thing that would tend to the further advancement of this society she would like to hear it. counselled them to speak their feelings and not be backward. Mother Morris bore her testimony also Sister Lynn. Said they desired to do the will of God, and to keep his commandments. Mother Willis & sister William [Ann] Haslam also bore their testimony Sister Hopkins said she would like to hear the sisters speak that had lately come in if there were any present. Sister Corey [Margaret Corry], Mother [Mary] Hunter, Mother [Ellen] Muir, Mother [Cynthia] Benson, Mother [Margaret] Bateman, & Mother [Ann] White bore their testimony and felt glad and thankful that they were here Mother Simpkins also bore her testimony and spoke in tongues. Sister Hopkins then called on sister Lily [Margaret Lillywhite] [p. [25]] who bore her testimony & expressed her thankfulness that she was gathered to the valleys of the mountains. It was moved and seconded that the following sisters become members of this Society. Sarah Urie, Elizabeth Haight, [blank] [Margaret] Keys, Roxsena R Patten, Margaret Lily, Emma Walker, Mary Lapworth. unanimously carried. Sister A Haight exhorted the sisters to not forget home manufacture. Sister Patten again spoke and expressed her feelings regarding this. Sister Hopkins informed the sisters where the treasury was and said if they had any patches or anything else to spare to take them there. Singing. Benediction by Sister Annabella Haight.

Ellen Lunt—Secretary [p. [26]]

---

As you can see from these entries, the female community at Cedar City were keen to have a role and a voice that could be heard. Ellen, who was in charge of the minutes, actually took all the pieces of paper and made them into one book using pasteboard that was carefully covered with some floral wallpaper to bookend them.

Regarding our main character Jonathan Pugmire Sr, these

entries, which mention a Sister Pugmire, suggest that one or both of his surviving wives Mary Baylis and Elizabeth South were part of the Ward Relief Society at this time.

---

*Jonathan Pugmire Sr*
Courtesy Leslie Ann Ballou

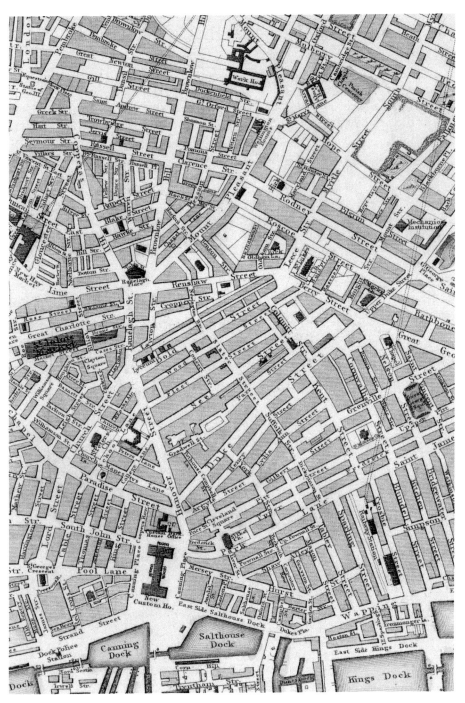

*Map of Liverpool in 1836, five years before the Pugmire family appeared in the 1841 census as living at Myrtle Street (shown top right)*

*Jonathan Pugmire Sr in later life*

*His friend, Thomas Cartwright*

*Jonathan Pugmire Jr*
*Courtesy Leslie Ann Ballou*

*Joseph Smith Jr, Founder of Mormonism*

*Salt Lake City*

# THE

# BOOK OF MORMON:

## AN ACCOUNT WRITTEN BY THE HAND OF MORMON, UPON PLATES TAKEN FROM THE PLATES OF NEPHI.

Wherefore it is an abridgment of the Record of the People of Nephi; and also of the Lamanites; written to the Lamanites, which are a remnant of the House of Israel; and also to Jew and Gentile; written by way of commandment, and also by the spirit of Prophesy and of Revelation. Written, and sealed up, and hid up unto the LORD, that they might not be destroyed; to come forth by the gift and power of GOD unto the interpretation thereof; sealed by the hand of Moroni, and hid up unto the LORD, to come forth in due time by the way of Gentile; the interpretation thereof by the gift of GOD; an abridgment taken from the Book of Ether.

Also, which is a Record of the People of Jared, which were scattered at the time the LORD confounded the language of the people when they were building a tower to get to Heaven: which is to shew unto the remnant of the House of Israel how great things the LORD hath done for their fathers; and that they may know the covenants of the LORD, that they are not cast off forever; and also to the convincing of the Jew and Gentile that JESUS is the CHRIST, the ETERNAL GOD, manifesting Himself unto all nations. And now if there be fault, it be the mistake of men; wherefore condemn not the things of GOD, that ye may be found spotless at the judgment seat of CHRIST.

---

## BY JOSEPH SMITH, JUNIOR.

AUTHOR AND PROPRIETOR.

---

## PALMYRA:

PRINTED BY E. B. GRANDIN, FOR THE AUTHOR.

## 1830.

*The 1830 publication of The Book of Mormon*

*The followers of Mormon.*

*Left to right from top left: Brigham Young, Thomas Dunlop Brown, William Law,*
*Sidney Rigdon, John Doyle Lee, Hyrum Smith,*
*Isaac C Haight, Philip Klingon Smith and Jacob Hamblin*

*Members of the travelling wagon party*

*The Meadow Mountains Massacre*

*Plaque for Jonathan Pugmire Sr at Salt Lake City Cemetery*
*Courtesy Chesnut/Behunin Descendant on findagrave.com*

# 30

# THE MOUNTAIN MEADOWS MASSACRE

*'There no longer remains any government in Utah but the despotism of Brigham Young'*

President James Buchanan

---

It was between the 7th and 11th September 1857 that a terrible, unimaginable massacre took place.

The following explains why such a thing could and did occur.

In 1857, the Mormon pioneer settlers at Utah including Jonathan Pugmire Sr and Thomas Cartwright were in a situation where they were increasingly pressured from the United States Government regarding Mormon practice and belief.

Aware of the hostility from outside the State, and under the guidance of their enigmatic and powerful leader Brigham Young, Pugmire, Cartwright and others found themselves enrolled into what became known as the Nauvoo Legion, the Mormon militia which had originated in Illinois but which had, 1857, relocated to Utah.

So it was that in September of 1857 the Mormon militia attacked the Baker-Fancher wagon train consisting of somewhere between 130 and 140 people who were travelling across the country to California. All of the people who made up the wagon train were killed, except for 17 children who were aged 11 years or younger.

In a Machiavellian twist, the massacre was made to look as if the Native American Indians of the Great Basin were responsible, and for a time it was indeed they who were blamed for everything that took place over those days in September

1857.

Subsequent reports of those five days in the Mountain Meadows included the name of Jonathan Pugmire amongst the list of those linked to the attack, although his actual involvement would appear less than that of his old friend from England, Thomas Cartwright, who seems to be more of an a active member.

―――――――

So what brought about the massacre?

Let me explain.

The Mountain Meadows Massacre came about partly because of the Utah War. This is the name given to a series of events that took place between May 1857 and July 1858. This war was between the Mormon pioneer settlers of Utah and the armed forces that represented the United States Government.

During this time the President of the United States, James Buchanan,[53] decided to send an army to the Utah territory in what would become known as the Utah Expedition, as he was concerned that the territory had fallen into lawlessness.

> Without entering upon a minute history of occurrences, it is sufficient to say that all the officers of the United States, judicial and executive, with the single exception of two Indian agents, have found it necessary for their own personal safety to withdraw from the territory, and there no longer remains any government in Utah but the despotism of Brigham Young.[54]

The Mormons were already aware how they were viewed from people outside of their faith, and feared that the army had come to destroy everything they were hoping to achieve.

Although the United States did not want a war, the Mormons

―――――――

53   The 15th President of the United States (1791-1868).
54   First Annual Message to Congress on the State of the Union by James Buchanan, 8th December 1857.

prepared themselves for battle. Under the leadership of Brigham Young, the followers of Jesus Christ of the Latter Day Saints viewed the state of Utah as a place where they could practice their beliefs with freedom, and be free from impunity.

The Nauvoo Legion repaired their faulty old firearms and fashioned farming tools into suitable weapons. They also actively blocked the US army from entering the Salt Lake Valley and made it hard for them to gather provisions that could sustain the troops that had been sent.

In the event, whilst there was friction between the Mormons and the US army, there was no actual war between the two sides other then some minimal damage to property.

For the Baker-Fancher wagon party who were travelling west through the area at the time, however, there would be a far less peaceful outcome. Nearly all of those passing through would be left for dead on the dust desert ground in Utah.

———————————

# 31

# THOSE INVOLVED
# IN THE MASSACRE

*'To the best of my recollection there were fifty-four white men
at the Mountain Meadows Massacre'*

John D Lee

---

There were three groups involved in the massacre of September 1857 that resulted in more than 100 people being killed:

- The Baker-Fancher travelling wagon party
- The Mormon Militia
- The Native American Paiute

---

## The Baker-Fancher Party

The Baker-Fancher party were a group of Arkansas emigrants consisting of wealthy farmers and cattle owners. They had gathered together all their belongings and set off in their wagons in April 1857 on a journey to California to begin a new life. As the name suggests, the wagon train was made up of the Baker party and the Fancher party.

The Baker train was overseen by Captain John Twitty Baker, who came from Carroll County, Arkansas. The Fancher train had Alexander Fancher as the leader. The actual number of people on the wagon train varied as they travelled towards California. Some of the smaller wagons left, whilst others joined. On leaving Arkansas, the number was thought to have been around 200 people.

Whilst on the long exodus to California the party would take part in prayer and religious gatherings under the guidance of fellow traveller, Methodist minister Pleasant Tackitt.

The Baker-Fancher party were not short when it came to wealth. The number of cattle they had taken with them on this journey amounted to around 1,000, and they also had plenty of horses and oxen. You may be wondering why, if they were already comfortable in Arkansas, they would then leave everything they had achieved and make this long journey.

History shows that some of the people who made up the party were simply wishing to begin a new and exciting life in California. Others were interested in taking cattle west to sell and make a profit and, if lucky, find out whether 'there's gold in them thar hills',[55] the California Gold Rush having begun eight years earlier.

These emigrants were not the first party to make the long journey to California. Like those who had gone before, all of the money they had earned and saved they took with them, along with all personal belongings. On Monday 7th September 1857, three months after setting off from Arkansas, the Baker-Fancher party decided to make a stop at Salt Lake City in order to stock up on supplies. The party assumed that filling their wagons here would see them through until they reached California.

This would prove to be a big mistake, as by the end of Friday 11th September around 120 of the party would be dead.

---

## The Mormon Militia

The exact number of men who attacked the wagon train as part of the militia is not known, although evidence suggests it was somewhere in the region of 50. At his trial, John D. Lee is quoted as saying:

'To the best of my recollection there were fifty-four white men

---

55  A quote in response to leaving for California by Colonel Mulberry Sellers, a character created by Mark Twain.

at the Mountain Meadows Massacre. The men who composed the preliminary council of war were these'.

The following is a list of some of the Militia recognised as being involved in the Mountain Meadows Massacre. This information comes from the recollections and testimony of John D. Lee at trials for the incident which took place in 1874 and 1877, and newspaper articles published after the event that reported on the massacre:

Isaac C Haight, a Major of the 2nd Battalion at Cedar City. Haight was one of the leaders at Cedar City who, after some debate, agreed to the attack of the wagon train.

John D Lee, a leader of the massacre who, as mentioned above, was eventually arrested for the crime.

William H Dame, Mayor of Parowan, Utah, who was prominently involved in the massacre.

John M Higbee.

Philip Klingon Smith.

Samuel Pollock, a Sergeant from Cedar City who was ordered to go to the Mountain Meadows.

Thomas Henry Cartwright, friend of Jonathan Pugmire Sr and a member of the 4th Platoon from Cedar City. Some years after the massacre Samuel Pollock recalled travelling with Cartwright to the Mountain Meadows.

Jonathan Pugmire Sr, mentioned in a report in the *New York Herald* of 22nd May 1877 as being one of approximately 50 Militia. He was named along with many others as a member by eyewitness accounts. The actual extent of his involvement, however, is not clear.

More about those people involved will be looked at later, when revisiting the Mountain Meadows.

---

## The Native American Paiute

According to scholars and historians the Paiutes, one of several groups of Native Americans that made up the indigenous people of the Great Basin, first set up home in what is now known as Utah sometime between 1100 and 1200 AD. For centuries, life with the Paiute revolved around hunting small animals, gathering plants and roots, farming corn and wheat and raising families.

In terms of a spiritual belief, the Paiutes looked to the Wolf and the Coyote. Seen as brothers, stories of both animals were often shared amongst families and their children in the long winter months.

The Paiutes had experienced some contact with Europeans from the 18th century onwards. One of the problems they encountered was the eating of crops planted for their families by the immigrants' hungry animals.

It was the arrival of the Mormons to Utah in the mid-19th century that impacted on their lifestyle the most, however.

By the 1850s the Paiute population decreased significantly as their traditional places to gather food and set up home were taken over by the arriving Mormons, who were seeking somewhere to establish a community following the death of founder Joseph Smith and subsequent hostility.

Under the leadership of Brigham Young, it was decided that Utah would be the place where they could preach the revelations of Smith and *The Book of Mormon*. This is why, in 1847, Jonathan Pugmire Sr and his family had made Salt Lake City their home, three long years after boarding that boat in far away Liverpool.

This claiming of the land around Salt Lake resulted in many Paiute, who had lived in the area for generations, succumbing to desperate starvation and disease.

––––––––––––––

Fast forward several years, and in 1857 the Mormon Militia approached the Paiute community to ask for help with a plan to stop the approaching Baker-Fancher wagon train that was heading for a new life in California, something of a brave move considering the Militia had taken over their land. It was proposed that together they could rob the travellers of all of their possessions.

––––––––––––––

# 32

# THE MASSACRE

*'Too young to tell tales'*

John M Higbee

---

At the beginning of September 1857 the Baker-Fancher wagon train party, which was by now made up of approximately 136 people, decided to stop their journey and attempt to gather some supplies at Salt Lake City. Having been travelling since April, a place where they could rest and let their cattle graze was the first priority. Unfortunately for the party the Mormon community, under the powerful leadership of President of the Church of Jesus Christ of Latter Day Saints Brigham Young, did not look favourably on wealthy travellers from Arkansas or their desire to reach California.

As the title of this chapter suggests, deciding to rest here would end in many, many deaths.

---

Let us begin on the morning of Monday 7th September 1857. Together with members of the Native American Paiute, the Mormon Militia set off to where the travelling party had set up their camp. The objective for the Militia and the Paiute was to take whatever valuables they could, by force if necessary. The Militia knew that the travellers had brought all of their money and valuable possessions with them.

The following description of what took place that September shows the Machiavellian ingenuity of the Mormon Militia as they put into practice what the leaders of their faith had decided they should do.

After travelling for several miles, the Militia arrived at the campsite where the Baker-Fancher party stopped for a brief rest. When the Militia arrived they did not look like themselves. Instead, they were all purposely dressed as members of the Native American Paiute tribe. The reason for this was quite clear: if anyone would be blamed for what may take place then it would be the Paiute people and certainly not the Mormon Militia, who had gone there confident of their disguise.

The approaching Native Americans would have of course alarmed the Baker-Fancher party who, in desperation and panic at the sight of the approaching Native Americans, tried to weigh down their wagons with dirt from the ground below, hoping to make them harder to remove. They protected their belongings like a mother would a child, although in this instance it would not prove successful. This first meeting ended with seven members of the Baker-Fancher party dead and 16 others injured.

The attack on the party would continue for five days in total. Whilst the Militia, still dressed as if part of the Paiute, were able to retreat to replenish supplies, the members of the Baker-Fancher wagon were not.

But the long duration of the ambush led to a disaster for the Mormon Militia. Some of the wagon party saw through the attempt to look like the Native American Paiute and became aware that it was actually the Mormons who were attacking them. This realisation soon reached Brigham Young and other members of the Militia back in Salt Lake City, which led to heated arguments with regard as to what they should do next. It is important to understand that the last thing they wanted was to be blamed for the attack.

After vigorous debate a decision was made and relayed to the Militia by John M Higbee:

Kill all the emigrants, with the exception of small children.[56]

Sources suggest that Higbee remarked that if the Native

---

56  *Massacre at Mountain Meadows*, New York. Oxford University Press (2008). A reported statement made by John M Higbee who was relaying information given to him by Haight and Dame whilst they were at the house of Jacob Hamblin.

Indians could not do it by themselves then they would need to be helped.[57]

---

This brings us to 11th September 1857. It was on this day that two members of the Mormon Militia carefully approached the Baker-Fancher wagon train. One of them had a white flag raised high above their head as a signal that they were coming in peace. Following several steps behind was one of the main members of the Militia, John D Lee, who explained that he had managed to organise a truce with the Paiute, so under the protection of the Mormons they would be escorted safely to the nearby town of Cedar City. The only caveat was that they gave up all their cattle and supplies to the Paiute.

The travelling wagon party agreed, and were then split into three groups. The youngest children and the injured remained in the wagons. The women and older children walked behind the wagons, with the men also walking behind accompanied on their right-hand side by armed Militia.

The travelling party remained in this position for some time, but the further they went the greater the distance between the three groups became as they negotiated shrubs and other obstacles. The small children and the injured in the wagons disappeared ahead, the women and older children followed some way behind, and the men were further back still.

What followed next was the mass murder at close range of over a hundred people who were looking to peacefully relocate in California.

Upon reaching a certain point the wagons containing the young and injured passed, and then, on the appearance of the next group of people, the Militia who were hiding with some of the Paiute Tribe revealed themselves and in a moment killed everyone nearby. Some members of the wagon train were able to run, although they were soon chased down and also killed.

---

57   *Massacre at Mountain Meadows*, Walker, Turley, Leonard. Oxford University Press.

Sara Frances Baker, who was one of the last survivors and a witness of what happened, wrote in detail about her experience many years later in an issue of *The American Weekly*, published on 25th August 1940:

> The Mountain Meadows Massacre:
> An Episode on the Road to Zion
> By Sara Frances 'Sallie' Baker Mitchell.

I've been interested in the series of articles running in *The American Weekly* about the Mormons, specially what has been said about the Mountain Meadows Massacre, way back in September 1857.

I'm the only person still living who was in that massacre, where the Mormons and the Indians attacked a party of 137 settlers on the way to California murdering everybody except 17 children, who were spared because they were all under eight years of age.

I was one of those children and when the killing started I was sitting on my daddy's lap in one of the wagons. The same bullet that snuffed out his life took a nick out of my left ear, leaving a scar you can see to this day.

Last November, I passed my 85th birthday and at the time of the massacre I wasn't quite three years old. But even when you're that young, you don't forget the horror of having your father gasp for breath and grow limp, while you have your arms around his neck, screaming with terror. You don't forget the blood curdling war whoops and the banging of guns all around you. You don't forget the screaming of the other children and the agonized shrieks of women being hacked to death with tomahawks. And you wouldn't forget it, either, if you saw your own mother topple over in the wagon beside you, with a big red splotch getting bigger and bigger on the front of her calico dress.

When the massacre started, Mother had my baby brother, Billy, in her lap and my two sisters, Betty and Mary Levina, were sitting in the back of the wagon. Billy wasn't quite two, Betty was about five and Vina was eight.

We never knew what became of Vina. Betty saw some

Mormons leading her over the hill, while the killing was still going on. Maybe they treated her the way the Dunlap girls were treated, later on I'm going to tell about the horrible thing that happened to them. And maybe they raised her up to be a Mormon. We never could find out.

Betty, Billy and I were taken to a Mormon home and kept there till the soldiers rescued us, along with the other children, about a year later, and carried us back to our folks in Arkansas. Captain James Lynch was in charge of the soldiers who found us, and I've got an interesting little thing to tell about him, too, when I get around to it.

But first I want to tell all I remember and all I've heard about the massacre itself, and what lead up to it.

My father was George Baker, a farmer who owned a fine tract of bottom land on Crooked Creek, near Harrison, Arkansas. He and my grandfather, like a lot of other men folks at that time in our part of the country, had heard so much about the California gold rush of 49 that they got the itch to go there. So my father and some of the other men from our neighborhood went out to California to look over the lay of the land and they came back with stories about gold that would just about make your eyes pop out.

There wasn't anything to do but for everybody in the family to pack up, bag and baggage, and light out for the coast. Everybody but Grandma Baker. She wouldn't budge. She put her foot down and said: «Arkansas is plenty good enough for me and Arkansas is where I'm going to stay." Her stubbornness saved her life, too, because if she had gone along she would have been killed, just as were all the other grown ups, including my grandfather, my father and mother and several of my uncles, aunts, and cousins. Our family joined forces with other settlers from neighboring farms under the leadership of Captain Alexander Fancher, and the whole outfit was known as Captain Fancher's party.

It wasn't made up of riff raff. Our caravan was one of the richest that ever crossed the plains and some people have said that that was one of the reasons the Indians attacked our folks to get their goods.

We traveled in carriages, buggies, hacks and wagons and

there were 40 extra teams of top notch horses and mules, in addition to 800 head of cattle and a stallion valued at $2,000. Altogether, the property in our caravan was valued at $70,000. Captain Fancher's party spent the Winter getting ready and when Spring came and everything was all set to go, John S. Baker, who was related to us, was sick with erysipelas and couldn't travel. So he and his family, along with some of his wife's relatives, waited a few days and then set out to overtake us. A number of times they came across places where we had camped and found the coals from our campfires still warm, but they never did catch up with us, and that is why they missed the Mountain Meadows Massacre but they ran into the tail end of the trouble, just the same, and had a terrible time themselves.

A lot has been said, both pro and con, about what caused the massacre. It wasn't just because we had a lot of property the Indians figured was well worth stealing. There were several other things that entered into it.

In the first place, the members of our party came from a section of the country not far from the district in Missouri and Illinois where the Mormons had been mighty badly treated. If you've been reading Mr. Robinson's articles in *The American Weekly*, you'll recall how the Mormons were driven out of Missouri into Illinois, where Joseph Smith, their Prophet and the founder of their religion, and his brother, Hyrum, were assassinated. Then they were driven out of Illinois and, after suffering all sorts of hardships crossing the plains, they finally got themselves established in Utah.

So, it is only natural that they should feel bitter about anybody who came from anywhere near the part of the country where they had had so much trouble. I'm sure nobody in our party had anything to do with the persecution of the Mormons in Missouri and Illinois, or anything to do with the assassination of Joseph Smith and his brother. But that didn't make any difference. The word got around, somehow, that somebody in our party was bragging about having in his possession the very same pistol that was used to kill the Mormon Prophet, and that he even said he aimed to use it on Brigham Young, who had taken over the leadership of the Mormons.

So far as I know there wasn't a word of truth in that, but the rumor got around, right after we reached Utah, and it made a lot of Mormons see red. Then somebody started working the Indians up against us, by telling them our party had been poisoning springs and water holes, to kill their horses. Now that just isn't so, nobody in our party would do a thing like that. Even if they had been mean enough, they wouldn't have been such fools as to do a thing like that in a country filled with Indians that were none too friendly to begin with. Then there was the fact that our party came from the same general district where Parley Pratt, a Mormon missionary, had been murdered by J. H. McLean, because Pratt had run away with McLean's wife and two small sons.

McLean didn't live in Arkansas. That just happened to be the place where he caught up with Pratt, after tracking him back and forth across the country. The McLeans lived in New Orleans , and in the Summer of 1854 Parley Pratt went there, hunting for new recruits, married women or unmarried women, it didn't seem to make much difference, so long as they would drop everything and follow him. I don't know why she did it, but Mrs. McLean listened to his arguments, took up with him, and ran away with him taking her two children with her.

Mrs. McLean took charge of the funeral. She got Blacksmith Wynn to order some boards, all planed and dressed, from a sawmill run by the father of John Steward, who was 16 at the time and afterwards became deputy sheriff of Crawford County, and the coffin was made out of them. Then young Steward hauled the body in the coffin out to the burial grounds in his daddy's ox cart. They didn't have any preacher. Mrs. McLean did the only talking that was done and among other things she said Pratt had been crucified.

After that, she went on to Salt Lake City , and nobody in our part of the country ever heard anything more about her. But early in 1857, just before our party set out for California, two Mormons showed up at Wynn's blacksmith shop and asked him a lot of questions. Then they turned back north, along the same route our party followed a few weeks later, and it certainly looks like those two Mormons found out that we were figuring on passing through Utah on our way to California and told the Danites, or Destroying Angels of the Mormons, to be on the lookout for us, because we were from the same district where Pratt was murdered.

At any rate, we sure did get a mighty unfriendly reception when we finally did reach Utah. By that time, the Mormons didn't have much use for anybody who wasn't a Mormon.

Off and on, ever since they took over Utah, the Mormons had been bickering with the Federal Government, insisting that they had a right to run everything to suit themselves. It finally got so bad President Buchanan issued an order removing Brigham Young as governor of the territory, and appointing Alfred Cumming to take his place. And just before we landed in Utah, the Mormons heard that Cumming was on his way out, backed up by an army of 2500 men. That made the Mormons mad as hornets, so mad, in fact, that Brigham Young issued a proclamation defying the Federal Government and proclaiming martial law, but the members of our party didn't know anything about that, and walked right into the hornet's nest.

When our caravan reached Salt Lake City in August, our supplies just about out, everybody tired and hungry, and our horses and cattle lean and badly in need of rest and a chance to graze, we were told to, move on and be quick about it. On top of that, the Mormons refused to sell us any food, that 's what I was told when I was growing up and I've always believed it was so.

So we had to move on, down to Mountain Meadows, in what is now Washington County, Utah. Mountain Meadows was a narrow valley, lying between two low ranges of hills, with plenty of fresh water, supplied by several little streams, and lots of grass for our stock to graze. So it looked like a good place for our party to rest up before tackling the 90 mile desert that lay just ahead. A lot has been written about what was going on among the Mormons while our party was resting at Mountain Meadows. Both sides of the question have been gone into pretty thoroughly, with a lot of arguments and evidence on each side, so anybody who wants to form his own opinion can took up the books on the subject and make his choice.

Some writers say that officials of the Mormon Church stirred the Indians up and kept egging them on till they attacked us, and then told their own folks to jump in and help the Indians finish up the job, after tricking our men into giving up their guns. But the Mormon writers insist that nobody with any real authority in the church organization knew what was going on till it was too late for them to stop it, even though they tried their best. They admit, though, that there were some Mormons mixed up in it, and years after it was over, they laid most of the blame on John D. Lee, who was a Mormon and an Indian agent. But I'll tell about that later. On the morning of September 7, our party was just sitting down to a breakfast of quail and cottontail rabbits when a shot rang out from a nearby gully, and one of the children toppled over, hit by the bullet.

Right away, the men saw they were being attacked by an Indian war party. In the first few minutes of fighting, twenty-two of our men were shot down, seven of them killed outright. Everybody was half starved to death and I reckon the whole crowd would have been wiped out right then and there if Captain Fancher hadn't been such a cool-headed man.

He had things organized in next to no time. All the women and children were rounded up in the corral, formed by the wagons, and the men divided into two groups, one to throw up breastworks with picks and shovels and the other to fire back at the Indians.

The fighting kept up pretty regularly for four days and nights. Most of our horses and cattle were driven away. Our ammunition was running out. We were cut off from our water supply. Altogether, it looked pretty hopeless but I don't think our men would have ever surrendered if John D. Lee and his crowd hadn't tricked them.

According to the way I heard it, while we were trapped down there in the valley, just about perishing for lack of water and food, John D. Lee and some of the other Mormons held a strange kind of prayer meeting back in the woods, just out of sight of our camp. They knelt down and prayed for Divine instructions, and then one of them named John M. Higbee, who was a major in the Mormon militia, got up and said: "I have evidence of God's approval of our mission."

He said all of our party must be put out of the way, and that none should be spared who was old enough to tell tales. Then they decided to let the Indians kill our women and older children, so no Mormon would be guilty of shedding innocent blood. They figured that more than likely all of our men were guilty of some sin or other, if it wasn't any thing worse than hating Mormons, and really should be killed, but maybe the women and older children were innocent of any wrong doing, and it seems Mormons prided themselves on being right scrupulous about shedding innocent blood.

Years later, when he was put on trial, John D. Lee insisted he was against the whole idea and tried to talk the others out of it, but that Major Higbee, Philip Klingensmith, who was a Mormon bishop, and some of the others told him he would have to go through with it, He said Higbee told him: "Brother Lee, I am ordered by President Haight to inform you that you shall receive a crown of Celestial glory for your faithfulness, and your eternal joy shall be complete."

I don't know whether or not that 's true, but that's what Lee said, and he claimed he had to follow orders because Haight was president of the Stake of Zion, or division of the church, at Cedar City.

But anyway, on the morning of September 11, John D. Lee and another Mormon came down toward our camp carrying a white flag and our men sent out a little girl dressed in white, to show that they were ready to come to terms.

Then Lee came on down to the camp and said the Indians had gone hog wild but that the Mormons would try to save us and take us all to Cedar City, the nearest big Mormon settlement, if our men would give up their guns.

Well, our men didn't have much choice. It was either stick it out and fight till the last of us was killed or starved, or else take Lee up on his proposition, even though it did sound fishy.

So the guns were all put in one wagon and sent on ahead. Then the wounded and the young children, including me, my two sisters and my baby brother were put in another wagon. My mother and father had been wounded during the fighting, so they were in the wagon with us children.

It's funny how you will recall unimportant details, after so many years. I remember, for instance, that the blankets we had with us in that wagon were bright red and had black borders.

After the wagon I was in had set out, the women and the older children followed us on foot. Then the Mormons made the men wait until the women and children were a good ways ahead before starting the men out single file, about ten feet apart. I think my grandfather must have been in that procession. Betty and I never could find out for sure just when he was killed, all we could learn was that he was killed during the massacre.

Each of our men had an armed Mormon walking right by his side. They said that was because the Indians might start acting up again, but that wasn't the real reason, as you will soon see.

The line had been moving along slowly for some little distance, when all of a sudden the figure of a white man appeared in the bushes with Indians all around him. I've heard that he was Higbee and that he shouted: "Do your duty!"

Anyway, the Indians opened fire and then charged down with their tomahawks. Each Mormon walking along with our men wheeled around suddenly and shot the man next to him, killing most of them on the spot.

The women and older children screamed at the top of their lungs and scattered every which way, but the Indians ran them down. They poked guns into the wagon, too, and killed all of the wounded. As I have already said, my father and mother were killed right before our eyes.

One of the Mormons ran up to the wagon, raised his gun and said: "Lord, my God, receive their spirits, it is for Thy Kingdom that I do this." Then he fired at a wounded man who was leaning against another man, killing them both with the same bullet.

A 14 year-old boy came running up toward our wagon, and the driver, who was a Mormon, hit him over the head with the butt end of his gun, crushing the boy's skull. A young girl about 11 years old, all covered with blood, was running toward the wagon when an Indian fired at her point blank.

In the midst of all the commotion, the two Dunlap girls I spoke about before, Ruth, who was 18, and Rachel, who was 16 made a wild dash for a clump of scrub oaks on the far side of a gully.

Hidden in the scrub oaks, they must have thought they were safe but they weren't. Their bodies were found later, and the evidence is that they suffered far worse than any of the other women.

John D. Lee confessed to a lot of things about the Mountain Meadows Massacre before he was finally executed for his part in it, but he never would admit that he had anything to do with what happened to the Dunlap girls. Just the same, a 16 year-old Indian boy, named Albert, who worked on the ranch of Jacob Hamblin, a Mormon who lived near the Meadows, said that he saw the whole thing and here's the way he told it:

Albert said another Indian found the girls, and sent for Lee. At first, Lee wanted to kill them then and there, because they were old enough to tell tales, but the Indian begged him to wait a while, because they were so pretty. Ruth was old enough to realize what that meant, so she dropped on her knees and pleaded with Lee to spare her, promising that she would love him all her life if he would.

But, according to Albert, Lee and that Indian mistreated those poor girls shamefully and then slit their throats.

I don't know whether or not Lee himself attacked the Dunlap girls and murdered them, or was directly responsible for what happened to them. But there doesn't seem to be much doubt that they were brutally mistreated by somebody, before being murdered just as Jacob Hamlin's Indian boy said they were. Hamblin was on his way back to his ranch from Salt Lake City at the time of the massacre and when he got home Albert told him about the Dunlap girls. Then the Indian boy led Hamblin to a clump of oak bushes not far from where the massacre took place and showed him the bodies of the two girls, stripped of all their clothing.

---

The Militia hurriedly buried the bodies of the dead where they fell, although the wind did not keep them hidden for long. Semi-exposed, many of the bodies of the wagon party eventually succumbed to the weather and local wildlife.

These terrible events at the Mountain Meadows would not end in success for the Militia, however.

There is always an aftermath.

---

# 33

# THE AFTERMATH

*'The children cruelly mangled and the most of them with their parents' blood still wet upon their clothes'*

Brevet Major J H Carleton

---

Immediately after the massacre, John D Lee, Isaac C Haight and Philip Klingensmith visited the leader and most important of all Mormons, Brigham Young, in Salt Lake City. They offered him the money they had taken from the pockets of the recent dead and asked what they should do with everything else they had taken.

Brigham Young's response on seeing them at his door may have been a surprise to the three of them. He said that he wanted nothing to do with what happened or any money they had taken. It is reported that John D Lee suggested the Native Indians would not be happy if they did not at least receive some of the cattle that were taken during the attack. After thinking for a moment, Young decided to leave it to Lee to sort out as he wanted to maintain a distance between himself and what had just taken place at the Mountain Meadows.

---

Jacob Piatt Dunn,[58] in his 1886 book *Massacres of the Mountains*, explained the aftermath:

> The bodies of the dead were searched by Higbee and Klingensmith, the Bishop of Cedar City, and the money

58   1855-1924.

found is supposed to have been kept by them. The remaining property was put in Klingensmith's custody temporarily, and afterwards, on instructions from Brigham Young, was turned over to Lee and sold by him for the benefit of the Church. The bodies were stripped entirely naked, and fingers and ears were mutilated in tearing from them the jewellery, to them no longer valuable. The bloody clothing and the bedding on which the wounded had lain were piled in the back room of the tithing-office at Cedar City for some weeks.

According to the American historian and author Juanita Brooks,[59] Brigham Young sent a report to the Commissioner of Indian Affairs in 1858 in which he outlined what had happened, claiming that it was the Native Americans who were responsible.

Whatever the reason and excuses made, one thing was clear; children were left without parents, Native Americans were blamed and many innocent people were hurriedly buried where they fell.

So it was that after the massacre John D Lee arranged for the children survivors to be taken to the nearby house of Mormon convert and missionary Jacob Hamblin[60] in Santa Carla, Utah. In his report on the incident, Brevet Major J H Carleton described the graphic scenes that Hamblin's wife was greeted with:

'Mrs. Hamblin is a simple-minded person of about 45, and evidently looks with the eyes of her husband at everything. She may really have been taught by the Mormons to believe it is no great sin to kill Gentiles and enjoy their property. Of the shooting of the emigrants, which she had herself heard, and knew at the time what was going on, she seemed to speak without a shudder, or any very great feeling; but when she told of the 17 orphan children who were brought by such a crowd to her own house of one small room there in the darkness of night, two of the children cruelly mangled and the most of them with their parents' blood still wet upon their clothes, and all of them

---

59   1898-1989. Brooks was a lifelong member of the LDS and had a keen interest in the Mountain Meadows Massacre.
60   Hamblin (1819-1886) would go on to give evidence at the 1877 trial of John D Lee.

shrieking with terror and grief and anguish, her own mother heart was touched. She at least deserves kind consideration for her care and nourishment of the three sisters, and for all she did for the little girl "about 1 year old who had been shot through one of her arms, the elbow, by a large ball, breaking both bones and cutting the arm half off".[61]

What becomes apparent is that immediately after the massacre the children were used as currency. They became a source of economic gain.

Jacob Piatt Dunn, in *Massacres of the Mountains*, recounted what happened to the remaining children following the attack:

> On June 29, seventeen of the children having been recovered, fifteen of them were sent East, overland, in spring-wagons, escorted by soldiers. Every possible provision was made for their comfort, and four women were sent with them to attend to their wants. Two boys about seven years of age, John C. Miller, known to the Mormons as John Calvin Sorel, and Milum Tackett, who was known to the Mormons as Ambrose Miram Taggit, were retained as witnesses. Those returned were Mary Miller, called by the Mormons Mary Sorel; William Tackett, known to the Mormons as William Taggit; Prudence Angeline Dunlap and Georgiana Dunlap, known to the Mormons as Angeline Huff and Annie Huff; Sophronia Jones, called by the Mormons Sophronia Huff; T. M. Jones, called by the Mormons Ephraim W. Huff; Kit Carson Fancher, called Charley Fancher by the Mormons; his cousin Tryphena Fancher, called Annie Fancher by the Mormons, and supposed by them to be Charley's sister; Betsy Baker, Sarah Jane Baker, William Baker, Rebecca Dunlap, Louisa Dunlap, Sarah Dunlap, and Joseph Miller, called by the Mormons Samuel Dunlap. They were met at Fort Leavenworth by Mr. Mitchell, whose great bereavement by

---

61   Special Report of the Mountain Meadows Massacre', by J. H. Carleton, Brevet Major, United States Army, Captain, First Dragoons.

this horrible affair has been mentioned. His little grandchild was not among the saved, as he had hoped.[62]

On a more optimistic note, two years after the massacre the surviving children were eventually reunited with their extended families.

Subsequent reports of what happened on the Mountain Meadows would include the name of Jonathan Pugmire Sr amongst the list of those linked to the attack.

---

62   *Massacres of the Mountains* by Jacob Piatt Dunn (NYC Harper & Bros) 1886, (p310).

# PART 3

# JONATHAN PUGMIRE SR: THE LATER YEARS

34

# THE PUGMIRES
# AFTER THE MASSACRE
# (1858-1876)

After the events that took place at the Mountain Meadows the
Pugmire family continued to make the best of things and serve
the Mormon community. What follows is a brief overview of the
extended Pugmire family during the years after 1857.

---

In 1858, not long after events at the Mountain Meadows,
Jonathan Pugmire Sr left Cedar City where he had been for
eight years and returned to Salt Lake City with his children and
two wives, Mary and Elizabeth.

By the end of 1859 his daughter Sarah, who had married
a man called Allen F Riley, found herself raising two young
children in the state of Missouri.

On 15th November 1861, Mary (Baylis Haywood) Pugmire
became the second of Pugmire's wives to die. Lancashire-born
Mary was 57 years of age and she was buried at the Salt Lake
City cemetery. Pugmire spent the rest of his life in Salt Lake
City with his third wife Elizabeth.[63]

Between 1860 and 1870 son Joseph Hyrum and his wife
Eleanor had five children together when living in Fillmore, a
place situated halfway between Cedar and Salt Lake City.

In 1865, Jonathan's second eldest daughter Elizabeth became
married to a man named Judah Jacob Joseph in California, later
going on to marry another man called Mortimer G. Taylor.

It was in 1868 that Jonathan's son Jonathan Jr moved to St

63   Elizabeth died on 4th April 1894 at Salt Lake City, Utah and was buried the following
     day.

Charles, Idaho, where he carried on his trade as a blacksmith and set up his own farm.

That same year eldest son George, who had chosen to stay in England when the Pugmire family departed, died in Liverpool at the age of 45. His wife Jane died seven years later in the same city.

In 1870 son Joseph Hyrum and his family also moved to St Charles, to be near where his brother Jonathan Jr had relocated. However, in 1871 Joseph and his family moved once more, this time to the state of Wyoming, where he had two more children. In 1875 Joseph and his large family moved once again and returned back to Utah.

It is also in 1870 where the American census shows Sarah and her husband Allen as living in Salt Lake City, parents at this time to seven children.[64]

Jonathan Pugmire Sr's youngest daughter, Mary Ann, would not be married for some time to come. Another of his daughters, Hannah, who would go on to marry several times. It was in 1870 when she gave birth in San Bernardino, California, to a daughter that she and her Illinois-born husband Beverly Collins Boren named Armenia Sarilda Boren. It is interesting to note that Beverly was 22 years older than Hannah.

The lives of the Pugmire children after 1876 will be discussed later on.

---

64   1870 Salt Lake City Ward 7, Salt Lake, Utah Territory Census.

# 35

# THE ELDERLY JONATHAN PUGMIRE SR

*'He frequently said to those who called to see him
that he would depart this life, and not recover'*

Jonathan Pugmire Jr

---

After the massacre it was important for those involved to maintain stability. Jonathan Pugmire Jr describes his life in Utah at before and after the time of the massacre:

> Early in 1849, I was, in connection with Thomas Tanner, called by President Brigham Young to work on the Public Works at blacksmithing. Brother Tanner and I were partners in blacksmithing. At the time we were called, Brother Tanner was appointed foreman, which position he held until his death in 1865. At his death I was appointed foreman and held that position until I left the employ in 1869. During the time of the move in 1858, I acted for a short time in the absence of D. M Wells as Superintendent of Public Works. While at Provo during the move, I assisted in erecting a public blacksmith shop, at which several of the old hands were employed. On the return of the people to Salt Lake City, President Brigham Young had a blacksmith shop erected, the building was 42 feet by 60 feet. I was made foreman. About 20 hands were employed in the shop.[65]

This personal description by Pugmire Jr shows that life for the Mormon community in Utah would continue.

---

65   *Heart Throbs of the West* (1947) by Kate B Carter.

On Wednesday 26th July 1876 Jonathan Pugmire Sr, older now and in ill-health, slowly leaned forward. He cast his gaze over several handwritten pages and, after taking a moment to deliberate, carefully and considerately signed his name at the bottom.

Jonathan had just signed his Will, and in just two weeks the blacksmith from Cumberland, England would look upon the earth one last time.

A friend called Henry Dinwoody,[66] aware of the condition that the older Pugmire was in, sent a telegram to Jonathan Pugmire Jr, explaining that Pugmire Sr's health was not good and that he should perhaps come and spend some precious time with his father, which he indeed did do.

At around this time, on learning of Pugmire's declining health, Brigham Young, asked for a meeting. This sad time was recalled by Jonathan Pugmire Jr:

> In the month of July, 1876, I received a telegram from Bro. Henry Dinwoody of Salt Lake City stating that my father was sick and that he requested me there. I immediately started for Salt Lake City and my arrival found my father as stated in the telegram. I stayed with my father and did all I could to make him comfortable seldom leaving his bedside until his death, which took place about 9 o'clock on the evening of the 9th of August 1876. Sometime before my father's death, Pres. Brigham Young sent for him to come to his office and ordained him to the office of Patriarch. My father departed this life without a struggle. He frequently said to those who called to see him that he would depart this life, and not recover.[67]

66  Born in Cheshire, England in 1825 and died in Salt Lake City, Utah in 1905.
67  Recalled by great granddaughter of Jonathan Pugmire Sr, Lucy Nebeker.

---

On Wednesday 9th August 1876, in Salt Lake City, Utah, our main character Jonathan Pugmire Sr, now an elderly man with wispy silver hair, drew one last breath.

---

The following is a contemporary announcement:

Jonathan Pugmire Sr died in Salt Lake City, Utah at 9pm on Aug 9 1876, from inflammation of the lungs at age 77. He was buried in the Salt Lake City Cemetery. His departure from this life was mourned by his family and a numerous circle of friends and acquaintances. Thus came to a close the life of a faithful and true Latter Day Saint who was ever ready to respond to the calls made upon him to assist in building up the great Latter Day Work, in which he was a firm believer.

---

# 36

# REVISITING THE MOUNTAIN MEADOWS

*'Thus, on the 10th day of September, 1857, was consummated one of the most cruel, cowardly and bloody murders known in our history'*

Mark Twain

---

Although Jonathan Pugmire Sr had died, the events in which he was involved still had implications and would continue to be discussed.

An example of this is highlighted by looking at the famous American author Mark Twain. Before he wrote of *Tom Sawyer* and the *Adventures of Huckleberry Finn*, Twain travelled through the United States of America and made notes on what he observed as he quietly studied the people he met along the way.

With regard to the massacre that occurred at the Mountain Meadows in 1857, Twain would not hold back on how he felt about what happened. The following passage is taken from his book *Roughing It*:[68]

> They professed to be on good terms with the Indians, and represented them as being very mad. They also proposed to intercede and settle the matter with the Indians. After several hours parley they, having (apparently) visited the Indians, gave the ultimatum of the savages; which was, that the emigrants should march out of their camp, leaving everything behind them, even their guns. It was promised by the Mormon bishops that they would bring a force and

---

68 First published in 1872.

guard the emigrants back to the settlements. The terms were agreed to, the emigrants being desirous of saving the lives of their families. The Mormons retired, and subsequently appeared with thirty or forty armed men. The emigrants were marched out, the women and children in front and the men behind, the Mormon guard being in the rear. When they had marched in this way about a mile, at a given signal the slaughter commenced. The men were almost all shot down at the first fire from the guard. Two only escaped, who fled to the desert, and were followed one hundred and fifty miles before they were overtaken and slaughtered. The women and children ran on, two or three hundred yards further, when they were overtaken and with the aid of the Indians they were slaughtered. Seventeen individuals only, of all the emigrant party, were spared, and they were little children, the eldest of them being only seven years old. Thus, on the 10th day of September, 1857, was consummated one of the most cruel, cowardly and bloody murders known in our history.

It was not until the 1870s and after the American Civil War when arrests were eventually made of the key Mormon Militia members involved in the massacre.

---

A 2002 article in the *Daily Telegraph* made a suggestion as to who was to blame for what took place at the Mountain Meadows, as new evidence had come to light:

A confession etched on a newly discovered lead sheet has shaken the Mormon Church by linking its revered leader, Brigham Young, with one of the worst massacres in American history.

The note claims that the founder of Salt Lake City ordered the 1857 Mountain Meadows Massacre, when a wagon train of 120 settlers, mostly women and children, were killed after they had thrown down their weapons on a promise of safe passage.

The Church of the Latter-Day Saints, as Mormons are properly known, first tried to blame Indians for the slaughter but after huge pressure from the federal government, John D

Lee, a militiaman who was Young's adopted son, was tried and executed 20 years later for organising the attack.

The Church has always maintained that the militia acted alone, despite persistent claims that documents incriminating its leaders were burned at the end of the 19th century. Schoolbooks in Utah do not mention the incident and it has been airbrushed out of the religion's official history.

The lead sheet is the first evidence to directly link the killings to Young, who is considered a modern-day prophet by Mormons after he led them on their trek across America to found the city at Salt Lake.

It was found during restoration work on the debris of Lee's Fort, the citadel at which Lee's militia forces were based on the Colorado River, under several inches of dirt and rat droppings in the main chamber.

It is signed by Lee, who had 19 wives and 64 children, and claims to be written "by my own hand", 15 years after the events it describes.

Filled with misspellings, grammatical errors and halted sentences, it says: "I do not fear athorty for the time is closing and am willing to take the blame for Fancher."

The wagon convoy was known as the Fancher party, after Alexander Fancher, who led it.

It continues: "Col Dane, Maj Higby and me - on orders from Pres Young thro Geo Smith took part - I trust in God - I have no fear - Death hold no terror."

The massacre occurred amid a climate of war hysteria as Utah's Mormons prepared for an invasion by federal troops, who had been dispatched to suppress the theocracy established in the region a decade earlier.

As the settlers' convoy entered the state en route from Arkansas to California, rumours spread that it contained men who had killed a Mormon leader and church leaders vowed vengeance.

After a five-day siege the Mormon militia sent in a party under a flag of truce and promised safe passage. When the "gentiles" left their encampment all but the youngest children were killed.

Historians were yesterday clamouring to examine the sheet, and tests were being conducted to determine where the lead was mined in an attempt to date it.

The possibilities of a forgery or a false claim by Lee have not been ruled out, but experts said that at the time that it was not unusual for people who wanted to preserve a record to etch it on lead.

Scott Fancher, a lawyer in Harrison, Arkansas, who is president of the Mountain Meadows Monument Foundation and a descendant of Alexander Fancher, welcomed the discovery as a significant step in forcing the Church to face up to the reality of its past behaviour. He said he had long believed that Young sanctioned the massacre as a demonstration to federal authorities that only he could control the Paiute Indians who supposedly took part in the attack.

"The only thing that surprises me is that it's taken this long to find the letter, not the admission of guilt or that Lee pointed the blame at Young," he said.

In Salt Lake City, Mormon leaders insisted that further checks had to be conducted on the authenticity of the note before it could be accepted as a historical document.

Dale Bills, a Mormon spokesman, insisted that Young did not order the killings although "some members of the faith acted independently at Mountain Meadows".

In 1999 work to restore a memorial at the settlers' burial site turned up bones and forensic tests showed many in the group had been shot and not bludgeoned to death by the Indians, who had no guns.[69]

---

Next we need to consider what part our protagonist Jonathan Pugmire played in the Mountain Meadows Massacre. Was he involved in the actual killing? Did he join in the shooting and clubbing? Or like several men that day, did he disobey orders and refuse to discharge his weapon?

69   Article by Oliver Poole in the *Daily Telegraph*, 27th February 2002.

In May 1877, the *New York Herald* and the *Salt Lake Daily Tribune* published the names of all the Mormon militiamen involved in the massacre. Their headlines were provocative:

'The Mormon Massacre:
Names of All the White Murderers'
*New York Herald*, May 22, 1877

'The Massacre:
The Names of All the Whites
Who Participated in It'
*Salt Lake Daily Tribune*, May 30, 1877.

Jonathan Pugmire's name appears in both newspaper reports. Commenting on this, author Richard E. Turley says:

> This list [of names], which claimed to be published posthumously from a handwritten note by John D. Lee, included several names that were not associated with other lists attributed to Lee, nor are the names verified from other sources. Those names, as listed in the article, are: J. [Jehiel] McConnel, "two men named Curtis," J. [Jonathan] Pugmire [Sr.], Sam Adair, Nate Adair, George Hanley [Hawley], Hairgraves, and William Hamblin. Ezra Curtis is known to have lived in southern Utah in 1857 and was identified as a massacre participant by eyewitness accounts. The name Hairgraves does not resemble the name of any known individual residing within the jurisdiction of the Iron Military District.[70]

In addition, David L. Bigler and Will Bagley supply the names of fifteen men who were reportedly involved in the massacre. Again, our leading character Jonathan Pugmire's name is mentioned:

> Among the men named in the *Cedar Stake Journal* [a church magazine], the following were reportedly at Mountain Meadows at the time of the massacre: Philip Klingensmith,

---

70  Ronald W. Walker, Richard E. Turley and Glen M. Leonard, *Massacre at Mountain Meadows* (Oxford University Press, 2008), p. 396.

John Higbee, William Bateman, John D Lee, Charles Hopkins, Samuel McMurdy, Daniel McFarlane, John Urie, William Tate, Richard Harrison, Nephi Johnson, Joel White, Ira Allen, Jonathan Pugmire and Eleazar Edwards.[71]

Although not definite, evidence clearly points to Jonathan Pugmire being present at Mountain Meadows on September 11. If he was there, then almost certainly he would have been ordered to take part in the massacre. That said, he would not have been the first soldier compelled to take part in atrocities against civilians.

Let us go back five days before the massacre began. Jonathan Pugmire attended a meeting of the Cedar City Council to discuss what action to take concerning the Baker-Fancher party passing through their territory. Some council members urged harsh measures, while others argued that the wagon train should be allowed to pass freely. Jonathan Pugmire was one of the firm voices calling for restraint: he spoke out against a violent course of action.[72] Therefore, it might be fair to conclude that if Jonathan Pugmire was involved in the massacre, it will only have been as an unwilling and appalled participant.

71  David L. Bigler and Will Bagley (eds), *Innocent Blood: Essential Narratives of the Mountain Meadows Massacre* (Spokane: Arthur H. Clark, 2008), p. 70.
72  Elias Morris, statement communicated to Andrew Jenson, 2 February 1892, Mountain Meadows Massacre File, LDS archives.

# 37

# THE NINE MEN OF
# THE MORMON MILITIA

*'I do not believe everything that is now being taught
and practiced by Brigham Young. I do not care
who hears it. It is my last word - it is so.'*

John Doyle Lee

―――――――――――――

In 1874 arrests were made of several of the key members of the
Mormon Militia involved in the 1857 massacre. Warrants were
also issued for some of the men who after what took place had
subsequently gone into hiding in order to avoid repercussions.

Nine warrants were issued in total, and the recipients are
listed below:

## John Doyle Lee (1812-1877)

It was John Doyle Lee, thought to have been the leader of
the Mormon Militia, who was first tried for the crimes of 1874.
This resulted in a hung jury. A second trial took place in 1877
and would be less favourable for him. He was singled out as the
leader of the massacre and sentenced to death. At the time Utah
law offered the guilty party a choice of execution; they could be
hung, shot or beheaded. John Doyle Lee opted to be shot.

Lee never denied knowledge of what happened back in
September 1857 at the Mountain Meadows. He did, however,
maintain that he killed no one.

It was on 23rd March 1877 that John Doyle Lee, one of the
pioneers of the Latter Day Saints movement and leader of
the attack, was taken and executed at the very spot where the

Mountain Meadows massacre took place 20 years before.

However, before the firing squad which had lined up opposite opened fire, Lee was asked if he had any last words. He took this opportunity, and feeling that he was being made into a scapegoat, stated:

> I am a true believer in the gospel of Jesus Christ. I do not believe everything that is now being taught and practiced by Brigham Young. I do not care who hears it. It is my last word - it is so. I believe he is leading the people astray, downward to destruction. But I believe in the gospel that was taught in its purity by Joseph Smith, in former days. I have my reasons for it. I studied to make this man's will my pleasure for thirty years. See, now, what I have come to this day! I have been sacrificed in a cowardly, dastardly manner. I cannot help it. It is my last word - it is so.[73]

Brigham Young, had his own views on Lee. He did not think the punishment for Lee was sufficient to allow him entrance into the celestial kingdom.

### William Horne Dame (1819-1884)

Dame was the administrator of the Militia and responsible for what they were directed to do. While he was not present when the attack took place, he visited the site the following day and is documented as saying, 'Horrible! Horrible!' Hearing this, the second in command, Isaac Haight, replied 'You should have thought of that before you issued the orders.'

In 1874, following the issues for arrest of those involved, Dame went into hiding. It was not long before he was apprehended and taken to jail in Utah to await charges. Fortunately for Dame, the charges against him were dropped in 1876. He was released and lived out the rest of his life in Parowan City, Utah where he died on 16th August 1884.

---

73   Juanita Brooks, *The Mountain Meadows Massacre* (Stanford University Press, 1950), pp. 151-52.

## Philip Klingensmith (1815-1881?)

Following the massacre Klingensmith left Utah and, except for a brief return to Parowan in the 1860s, never returned. What he did do, however, was to tell all about what happened and those who were involved.

On 10th April 1871, following an interview with Charles Wandell, a long-standing Mormon follower who had visited Utah to discover what had happened at the Mountain Meadows. the following affidavit by Klingensmith was produced:

My name is Philip Klingon Smith; I reside in the county of Lincoln, in the State of Nevada; I resided at Cedar City in the County of Iron, in the Territory of Utah, from A.D. 1852 to A.D. 1859; I was residing at said Cedar City at the time of the massacre at Mountain Meadows, in said Territory of Utah; I had heard that a company of emigrants was on its way from Salt Lake City, bound for California; after said company had left Cedar City, the militia was called out for the purpose of committing acts of hostility against them; said call was a regular military call from the superior officers to the subordinate officers and privates of the regiment at Cedar City and vicinity, composing a part of the militia of the Territory of Utah; I do not recollect the number of the regiment. I was at that time the Bishop of the Church of Jesus Christ of Latter-day Saints at Cedar City; Isaac C. Haight was President over said church at Cedar City and the southern settlements in said Territory; my position as Bishop was subordinate to that of said President. W. H. Dame was the President of said Church at Parowan, in said Iron County, said Dame was also colonel of said regiment; said Isaac C. Haight was lieutenant-colonel of said regiment, and said John D. Lee, of Harmony in said Iron County, was Major. Said regiment was duly ordered to muster, armed and equipped as the law directs, and prepared for field operations. I had no command nor office in said regiment on the expedition which resulted in said company's being massacred in the Mountain Meadows, in said County of Iron. About four days after said company of emigrants had left Cedar City, that portion of said regiment then mustered at Cedar City took up its line of march in pursuit of them. About two days after said company had left Cedar City, Lieutenant-Colonel I. C. Haight expressed in my presence a desire that said company might be permitted to pass on their way in peace; but afterward he told me that he had orders to kill all of said company of emigrants except the little children. I do not know whether said headquarters meant the [regional] headquarters at Parowan or the headquarters of the Commander-in-chief at Salt Lake City. When the said company had got to Iron Creek, about twenty miles from Cedar City, Captain Joel White started for Pinto Creek Settlement, through which the said company would pass for the purpose of influencing the people to permit said company to pass on their way in peace. I asked and obtained permission of said White to go with him and aid him in trying to save life. When we got about three miles from Cedar City, we met Major J. D. Lee, who asked us where we were going. I replied that we were going to try to prevent the killing of the emigrants, Lee replied, "I have something to say about that." Lee was at that time on his way to Parowan, the headquarters of Colonel Dame. Said White and I went to Pinto Creek; remained there one night, and the next day returned to Cedar City, meeting said company of emigrants at Iron Creek. Before reaching Cedar City we met one Ira Allen, who told us that "The decree had passed devoting said company to destruction." After the fight had been going on for three or four days a messenger from Major Lee reached Cedar City, who stated that the fight had not been altogether successful, upon which Lieutenant-Colonel Haight ordered out a reinforcement. At this time I was ordered out by Captain John M. Higby who ordered me to muster, "armed and equipped as the law directs." It was a matter of life or death to me to muster or not, and I mustered with the reinforcing troops. It was at this time that Lieutenant-Colonel Haight said to me that it was the orders from headquarters that all but the little children of said company were to be killed. Said Haight had at that time just returned from headquarters at Parowan, where a military council had been held. There had been a like council held at Parowan previous to that, at which were present Colonel Dame, Lieutenant-Colonel I. C. Haight and Major John D.

Lee. The result of this first council was the calling out of said regiment for the purpose already stated.

The reinforcement aforesaid was marched to the Mountain Meadows, and there formed a junction with the main body. Major Lee massed all the troops at a spring and made a speech to them, saying that his orders from "headquarters were to kill the entire company except the small children." I was not in the ranks at that time, but on the side talking to a man named Slade, and could not have seen a paper in Major Lee's hands. Said Lee then sent a flag of truce into the emigrant camp, offering said emigrants that "if they lay down their arms, he would protect them." They accordingly laid down their arms, came out from their camp, and delivered themselves to said Lee. The women and children were then, by the order of said Lee, separated from the men and were marched ahead of the men. After the said emigrants had marched about a half mile toward Cedar City the order was given to shoot them down. At that time said Lee was at the head of the column. I was in the rear. I did not hear Lee give the order to fire, but heard it from the under officers as it was passed down the column. The emigrants were then and there shot down, except seventeen little children, which I immediately took into my charge. I do not know the total number of said company as I did not stop to count the dead. I immediately put the little children in baggage wagons belonging to the regiment and took them to Hamblin's ranch, and from there to Cedar City, and procured them homes among the people; J. Willis and S. Murdy assisted me in taking charge of said children. On the evening of the massacre W. H. Dame and Lieut. I. C. Haight came to Hamblin's, where I had said children, and fell into a dispute, in the course of which said Haight told Colonel Dame, that, if he was going to report of the killing of said emigrants he should not have ordered it done. I do not know when or where said troops were disbanded. About two weeks after said massacre occurred said Major Lee (who was also an Indian agent) went to Salt Lake City and, as I believe, reported said fight and its results to the commander-in-chief: I was not present at either of the before-mentioned councils, nor at any council connected with the aforesaid military operations or with said company. I gave no orders except to those connected with the saving of the children, and those, after the massacre had occurred, and said orders were given as bishop and not in a military sense. At the time of the firing of the first volley I discharged my piece. I did not fire afterwards, though several subsequent volleys were fired. After the first fire we delivered I at once set about saving the children. I commenced to gather up the children before the firing had ceased. I have made the foregoing statements before the above-entitled Court for the reason that I believe that I would be assassinated should I attempt to make the same before any court in the Territory of Utah. After said Lee returned from Salt Lake City, as aforesaid, said Lee told me that he had reported fully to the President, meaning the commander-in-chief, the fight at Mountain Meadows and the killing of said emigrants. Brigham Young was at that time the commander-in-chief of the militia of the Territory of Utah; and further deponent saith not.

This was the first public declaration of responsibility by any of those involved. The statement was initially published by Wandell in the *Daily Corinne Reporter* of 20th September 1872, and it did not take long for news of this statement to reach Utah, where it was published the following year. His affidavit caused quite a stir and led to a renewed desire by the public to hold those involved in the Mountain Meadows massacre accountable.

Klingensmith himself went on to testify against John D Lee in the 1875 trial in order to escape the death penalty. Shortly after this he disappeared. It is not known where he went, although some reports suggest he went first to Arizona and then on to Mexico, where he died some time after 1881.

One such report comes from the *Salt Lake Daily Tribune* of 4th August 1881:

### KLINGENSMITH
He is Supposed to Have Been Murdered by Mormons.

News has reached Pioche, says the Record, that bishop Philip Klingensmith, at one time a man of high standing and great influence in the Mormon Church, and the exposer of the

Mountain Meadows massacre, and the names of the men who participated in the bloody deed, is dead. His body was found in a prospect hole, in the State of Sonora, Mexico, and a letter from there, which was received in the vicinity of Pioche, states that the mystery surrounding the body indicates that Klingensmith had been murdered. Klingensmith died just as he expected, for on his return from Beaver in 1875, after testifying in the trial of John D. Lee, we met Klingensmith in town, in a sort of secluded spot, and during the conversation Klingensmith remarked: "I know that the Church will kill me, sooner or later, and I am as confident of that fact as I am that I am sitting on this rock. It is only a question of time; but I am going to live as long as I can." Immediately after Klingensmith's return from Lee's trial, as his wife at Panaca refused to have anything to do with him, being so ordered by the Church, he started southward and lived in Arizona for a while following prospecting. During his residence in the mountains of that Territory two attempts were made upon his life, but by whom he never was able to discover. Klingensmith made the exposure of the butchery at Mountain Meadows more for self protection than anything else. In early days, when Hiko was the county seat of Lincoln and the flourishing and only prominent mining camp in this southern country, the Mormons used to haul all the freight from Salt Lake to Hiko. Klingensmith was engaged in freighting, and his son, Bud Klingensmith, was assisting him. During one of these trips father and son had [a] quarrel and Bud went to Hiko and obtained employment. It was during the winter of 1867-68, when Klingensmith arrived in Hiko with a load of freight, his son pointed him out to the people, and told them that just after the massacre he pointed out a young girl to him and ordered him to kill her, saying that if he (Bud) did not kill her he (his father) would kill him." Then Bishop Klingensmith turned upon the poor girl himself and knocked her brains out with a club. This was the first inkling to anything authentic in connection with the massacre, and caused considerable excitement among the settlers of Hiko. Wandell, one of the county officials at that time informed Bishop Klingensmith what his son exposed, and hurried him out of town. After that, while engaged in handling freight, upon his arrival at Panaca, Klingensmith would always hire some one to drive his team over to Hiko. In 1871 Bishop Klingensmith made affidavits before the Clerk of Lincoln county, making the exposure of the massacre, and the names of those connected therewith, which was published in the Record and made public for the first time. Mrs. Klingensmith is now living at Bullionville, and is married to a man named Dolf Laundrich. Mrs. Klingensmith is an intelligent old lady, and is the mother of seventeen children by Klingensmith, the last two being girls, who are now about sixteen years of age. Most of the Klingensmith family reside in Lincoln county.

There was always something incomprehensible about Klingensmith and the actions and exposures of the Mountain Meadows massacre. In the first place it is remarkable that he should have told his story at all, for he possessed no such keenness of conscience as would compel him to divulge the crime as an act of justice to the world.

Then, when he did tell it, he never would tell it all, but stopped just where it was most desirable that he should continue; again, he never told the story alike any two tellings, and it always stopped just short of being legally conclusive against any person. That he professed fear of his life on account of what he had told is certain, that he actually felt and realized such fear is not so certain. When he was found in 1875, and brought to Utah as a witness in the second Lee trial, he was living with two Indian squaws near the river, below Ehrenburg, Arizona. He was with some difficulty persuaded to come after being assured the fullest protection against the Mormon violence he professed to fear. On leaving Beaver, however, he requested not to be returned by the safe way he had come, but desired to have a horse, saddle and traveling outfit, and on being supplied he struck off through the southern Mormon settlements to go back to Ehrenburg by the southern overland trail, alone and unprotected, as he had asked to do, thereby ignoring the very protection he had insisted upon. That did not look as if he had any particular fear of assassination at that time, whatever he may have really felt at other times. He was certainly a most reckless liar, and probably a cruel villain, who did his full share of the bloody work at the Meadows. If he was really killed by the Mormons at the last, all we have to say is, they waited an unconscionable while before taking their revenge upon him and missed many a good and more convenient opportunity than that of which they finally availed themselves.

In this connection we publish the following letter, just received:

Dillon, M. T., July 30, 1881.

Eds. Tribune. I see by an item in the Ogden Pilot of the 27th inst., a notice of the death of Phillip Klingensmith, and referring to the Tribune from which the item was taken. I write now to ascertain how the news was obtained and all the particulars. He was my brother, and I have a deep interest in knowing all about his death, which I have long expected at the hands of the Mormons. Very truly, Mrs. D. H. Simmons.

## Ellott Willden (1833-1920)

English-born Willden was baptized into the Mormon faith in 1845. He was named as someone who had participated in the Mountain Meadows massacre, and an arrest warrant was issued in 1859.

In 1874 he found himself one of the nine members of the Militia who were indicted for murder. He was released on bail however, and all charges were eventually dismissed. Following the trial Willden married again and would go on to make a life for himself in Beaver County, Utah.

## George Adair Jr (1837-1909)

Rather than blaming the Paiute Indians for the killing of women and children, Adair, whilst in drink, happily told all about his fellow militiamen and their exploits. Contemporary reports at the time suggest he was pleased with how he murdered the members of the wagon train.

This role of Adair is discussed in a website called 'Legends of America':

Though there were numerous privates in the Iron Militia that were never indicted, the young Adair, who was allegedly a heavy drinker, brought attention to himself in the streets of Cedar City, by boasting about the killings.

Laughingly, he was said to have imitated how he had taken babies by their heels, swinging them into the iron bands of the wagon wheels, crushing the skulls in the process. Private Adair was arrested and jailed for six months before he was released on bail on May 12, 1876. When U.S. S. Attorney Sumner Howard recommended to Adair that he plead guilty to the charges against him, Adair allegedly responded, "I'll see you in Hell first!" Unfortunately, the charges were never followed through with Adair.[74]

Adair died in San Juan County, New Mexico on 9th September 1909.

## Isaac Chauncey Haight (1813-1886)

Following the Civil War in America, investigations once again looked into what happened at Mountain Meadows. Haight was identified as one of the leaders, and the one who gave the order to attack the Baker-Fancher party.

In 1870, following public anti-Mormon pressure Haight was excommunicated from the Church. Four years later, in 1874, Brigham Young reinstated him back into the embrace of the Mormon Church.

It was this same year when a warrant was issued for his arrest over his involvement in the massacre. Fearing retribution Haight went into hiding and changed his surname to Horton (his mother's maiden name). He relocated to Arizona and set up home in the town of Thatcher. This was where he remained for the next 12 years, before he died on 8th September 1886.

## John Mount Higbee (1827-1904)

Higbee was one of the first people at Mountain Meadows and arranged for messages to be sent back to Cedar City regarding

---

74 www.legendsofamerica.com/ut-mountainmeadowsassassins2.html

the wagon train party that had stopped there. He blamed John D Lee for giving the go-ahead for the massacre, and in turn John D Lee pointed the blame to him.

Not wishing to be tried in for the crimes, in 1874 he took the same decision as fellow members and indicted Isaac C Haight and William C Stewart and went into hiding. By the 1880s, with public demand to have those brought to account diminishing, Higbee felt safe from being called to account for his involvement. He went on to spend the next 20 years with his two wives and their many children. Higbee was the last surviving member of the nine when he died in 1904 at the age of 77.

## William C Stewart (1827-1895)

Scottish-born William Stewart, who was known as Bill, converted to Mormonism back in Britain. By the 1850s he was an important member of the Cedar City community. On 7th September 1857, along with around 25 armed men he left on horseback and headed to the Mountain Meadows. Involved in the altercation that took place, Stewart fired shots and killed multiple people.

Fellow member of the Militia Ellott Willden described how Stewart was so enthusiastic he chased someone for 100 yards before killing them. John D Lee would attest that it was Stewart, along with John Higbee and Philip Klingensmith, who searched the bodies for any valuable possessions.

## Samuel Jewkes (1823-1900)

In 1855 the Mormon convert Samuel Jewkes, who had been born in Staffordshire, England, found himself far across the Atlantic in Cedar City, Utah. His involvement at Mountain Meadows is unclear. He was, however, indicted along with eight other men to stand trial.

Jewkes died in Emery County, Utah on 21st August 1900, and was survived by two wives and eight children.

# 38

# THE CHILDREN OF
# THE MOUNTAIN MEADOWS

The following article comes from *The Modesto Bee*, a local newspaper distributed in Turlock, California. The specific article relevant to this story was published on 10th May 1940:

### LAST SURVIVOR OF MASSACRE
### IS CALLED BY DEATH

TURLOCK, May 10 - William Tillman Miller, 84, believed to be the last survivor of the Mountain Meadows massacre which took place in Utah in 1857, died in the home of his son here this morning.

The massacre occurred when Miller was 6 months old. He and approximately twenty other small children were the only persons spared by a Mormon tribe which sought to avenge the killing of one of their number in Arkansas earlier the same year.

Miller was with his parents, who were traveling from Arkansas and had camped near Mountain Meadows, Washington County, Utah, on their way to California.

Miller came to California fifty two years ago, settling first in San Bernardino County, and had lived in Turlock for the past nine years. He leaves four sons, Claude E. Miller of Turlock, Thomas Miller of Wasco, Joseph F. and E. E. Miller, both of Los Angeles; two daughters, Mrs. Mary Stohr of Compton and Mrs. Nettie Warrecker of Santa Ana, and one stepson, Frank Boyd of Fellows. His wife died in 1932.

Funeral services will be conducted in the J. W. Guy Funeral Chapel at 10:30 o'clock Monday morning with Rev. Laurence C. Sunkler, pastor of the First Christian Church, officiating. Interment will be in the Turlock Cemetery'.

---

The next article is taken from the *Turlock Tribune* and was published on 17th May 1940:

Colorful Pioneer Dies Here At 84

The frontiers of America have disappeared, they say, and whether that is true or not, certain it is that the old frontiersmen of America are disappearing from the scenes of their adventures.

William Tillman Miller of Turlock was dead today, and with his death there passed one of the last of the old pioneers who blazed a trail westward across a continent, and the sole survivor, it is believed, of the historic Mountain Meadow Massacre in Utah in 1857.

Miller, a retired rancher, was 84. He died Friday at his home at 313 Boulevard Street here. He had lived in Turlock for the past nine years.

There is no record of Miller's place of birth. According to historical legend, however, he, as an infant child, was a member of the caravan of Arkansas travelers who trekked into Utah in 1857 only to meet death at the hands of the followers of Brigham Young.

Utah, at that time, was considered sacred soil by the Mormons the holy ground of the Territory of Deseret.

Miller (it was reported) was a member of a caravan of about 120 men, women, and children who traveled to Utah by covered wagon from Arkansas, on the way to California. At Mountain Meadow, history records, they pitched their camp and were spied by Mormon agents.

According to legend, Young had sworn to punish with death all interlopers who set foot in Utah as a result of the slaying of the Mormon leader, Parley Parker Pratt, near Van Buren, Ark., on May 13, 1857.

Pratt had eloped with the wife of Hector H. McLean, it is recorded, and was slain by McLean.

According to one account of the battle, the Mormons used typical twentieth-century Trojan horse or fifth-column strategy in wiping out the encampment of Arkansas pioneers.

The group from Arkansas formed a semi-circle with their

covered wagons and converted the assembly into a rude fort.

When the Mormons attacked, a volley of rifle fire drove them off.

Then, according to the account, agents of the Mormons came to the Arkansas camp bearing a white flag. They were admitted and told the beleaguered travelers that federal soldiers had come to their rescue.

The Arkansans, according to the account, believed them, laid aside their arms, and followed the Mormons out of their hastily erected fortress.

When the group reached a certain point, the Mormons opened fire. The camp then was stormed. According to one account of the massacre, only a few children, of whom Miller was one, were saved. These were adopted, placed in Mormon homes, from which they were taken when federal troops took the situation in hand after authorities had been informed of the battle.

Miller's parents, two aunts and an uncle were slain in the battle, according to reports.

From Utah Miller was taken to Kansas, later went back to Texas, in 1876 he and his wife came to California, established their residence at Colton and lived in Los Angeles and Southern California until moving to Oakland where he resided until coming to Turlock.

Miller's wife, Brancy Ann Miller, died in 1932. Survivors include four sons, Claude Elmer Miller of Turlock, Thomas T. Miller of Wasco, Calif., Joseph F. Miller and E. E. Miller, both of Los Angeles; two daughters, Mrs. Nellie Warrecher of Santa Ana, and Mrs. Mary Stohr of Compton; and a step-son, Frank Boyd of Fellows, Calif.[75]

---

So what happened to all of the children whose lives were spared during the massacre of 1857?

75  *Turlock Tribune*, 17th May 1940.

## John Calvin Miller

Following the massacre, John and his younger brother Joseph were sent to live with the Groves family in Harmony, Utah.

In 1859, John and fellow survivor Emberson Milum Tackitt were taken to the capital, Washington DC, to explain what happened at the Mountain Meadows to the Government. No records have been found of what was said.

In the US census of 1860 John Calvin, by then 9-years-old, was living with an attorney called William W Watkins and his family in Carroll County, Arkansas.

## George Ann Dunlap

A baby at the time, George Ann was born on 1st February 1857 to Lorenzo and Nancy Jane Dunlap. Six of her seven elder siblings were killed, along with her parents.

The recollections of George Ann's uncle in relation to his nieces was recorded by a diarist named Silas Claiborne Turnbo:[76]

> Among the little children who were spared a horrible death on that bloody spot were Angeline and George Ann Dunlap two daughters of my brother Loranzo Dunlap and Louisa. Sarah and Rebecca Dunlap daughters of my brother Jesse Dunlap. All of these children that I name were married after they grew to womanhood. Angeline married Blairburne Copeing, George Ann married George McWhister, Louisa married Jim Linton, Rebecca married John Evans and Sarah married Capt. Lynch of the United States Army.[77]

## Emberson Milum Tackitt

Immediately following the attack, Emberson and his brother William were placed with a Mormon family at Cedar City, Utah. It would be two years before the brothers were reunited with family members, and raised by their maternal grandparents in

76   1844-1925.
77   Five Children Who Were Saved from the Mountain Meadow Massacre by diarist S. C. Turnbo.

Carroll County, Arkansas.

By the time Emberson reached adulthood he had moved to Prescott, Arizona where he served as a deputy sheriff. It was there that he died on 12th June 1912 from tuberculosis. He may have been married at one point, as his obituary states that he had a son called Edward.

### Mary Miller

Mary was separated from her two brothers, John and Joseph, and sent to live with a man called John Morris and his family in Cedar City, Utah. By 1859 she was reunited with her brothers and living with an aunt in Crawford County, Arkansas.

### William 'Joseph' Tillman Miller

Joseph, who was only a year old at the time of the massacre, was sent with his older brother John to a family in Harmony in Utah, before being taken in by an aunt along with his sister Mary.

Joseph grew up in Crawford County before leaving for Texas where he became a rancher and married a woman called Brancy Ann Miller. in 1876 they left for California, where they raised six children. Brancy died in 1932 and Joseph in 1940 aged 84.

### Prudence Angeline Dunlap

Prudence, the seventh of eight children, was born on 9th of January 1852. She witnessed the murder of her parents Lorenzo and Nancy Dunlap and six older siblings. Only she and younger sister George Ann were spared. Following the massacre, the two surviving girls were separated before being later reunited and raised by a friend of their fathers. Prudence went on to marry and raise a family in Texas. She died on 5th November 1918 in Mills County, Texas.

### Sara Frances Baker

Sara, known as Sallie, was born in 1854 in the State of

Arkansas. Both her parents and older sister were killed at the Mountain Meadows. She survived, as did her sister Martha and brother William. After the massacre Sara was separated from her brother and sister. It would be two years before she was reunited with them in Arkansas.

Sara was one of the last surviving members of the wagon train that was attacked back in 1857. In 1940, at 85-years-old, she wrote in detail of what happened at the Mountain Meadows in *The American Weekly* magazine.[78] The following extract describes what happened after the massacre:

> In the Spring of 1859, Major James H. Carleton passed through Mountain Meadows and stopped there long enough to gather up the bones of the victims of the massacre. He found 34 skeletons and buried them in one place, under a heap of stones, and put up a cedar cross with these words on it: "Vengeance is Mine; I will repay, saith the Lord."
>
> Later on, Captain R. P. Campbell passed through the Meadows and found 26 more skeletons, which he also buried there. That only accounts for about half of the victims. Nobody knows what became of the other bodies.
>
> In later years, a granite slab was put up in the Meadows, and on it were these words: "Here one hundred and twenty men, women and children were massacred in cold blood in September, 1857. They were from Arkansas."
>
> Long after I had grown up and married and settled down, Captain Lynch, the man who rescued us, came to see me one day. He was in mighty high spirits and I could see right away he had something up his sleeve. He asked me if I remembered little Sarah Dunlap, one of the children he had rescued, and a sister of the two Dunlap girls who were killed. I said I sure did. Sarah was blind and had been educated at the school for the blind in Little Rock . I don't recall whether any injury she might have gotten in the massacre was what made her blind, but I do remember she grew up to be a really beautiful girl. Well, Captain Lynch said: "Guess what? I'm on my way to see Sarah."

---

78 *The American Weekly*, 25th August, 1940.

When he mentioned her name it looked like he was going to blow up with happiness. Then he told me why. He was on his way right then to marry Sarah, and he did. I guess he must have been forty years older than she was, but he sure was a spry man just the same. I never saw anybody could beat him when it came to dancing and singing.

Some time after the massacre, Federal Judge Cradlebaugh held an investigation and tried to bring to trial some of the Mormons. He was convinced they were responsible for the crime, but he never got anywhere with it, and he was finally transferred from the district at his own request. Then the Civil War came on and nothing more was done about it until 1875.

## Felix Marion Jones

Felix was just 18-months-old when the massacre took place. After his parents and older sister were killed, he was taken in by a Mormon family before being taken back to his home state of Arkansas.

On 19th January 1882 Felix married Martha Ann Reed in Copperas Cove, Texas. They went on to have five children together. Felix died on 31st May 1932 in the same place where he was married; Copperas Cove, Texas.

## William Henry Tackitt

As he was just a baby, William was spared along with his brother Emberson and after two years was reunited with family members, being raised by their mother's parents. As an adult William went on to marry and moved to the state of Missouri, where he died in 1891.

## Christopher Carson Fancher

Christopher who was know as, 'Kit', was the second youngest child of wagon leader Alexander Fancher and his wife Eliza. With his sister Tryphena he watched as their family were murdered.

Christopher was 20-years-old when he died. He never married and is buried in Osage, Arkansas.

### Nancy Saphronia Huff

Nancy was born in 1853 in Arkansas. Her father Peter was the only person on the wagon train that was travelling through Utah to die before the actual massacre took place, succumbing to a spider bite before what would take place at Meadow Mountains. He was buried in Fort Bridger, Wyoming. Salidia Brown Huff, Nancy's mother, was killed in the massacre.

After the attack Nancy was sent to live with a Mormon by the name of John Willis in Cedar City, Utah. Eventually she was sent to stay with her grandfather. In 1875 she married a man called Dallas Cates and the couple set up a home in Yell County, Arkansas.

Tragically for Nancy, she was only about 25-years-old when she died in 1878 in Perry County, Arkansas. She was buried in the local Antioch cemetery.

### Martha Elizabeth Baker

Martha was around 5-years-old at the time of the attack. On 24th January 1874 she married J W Terry and together they raised nine children. Her husband died in 1927. In 1938 reporter Clyde R Greenhaw of the *Arkansas Gazette* met with Martha, who was now well into her eighties, to discuss what happened at the Mountain Meadows all those years ago. She would recollect how her parents, grandfather, uncle and aunts were all killed and that she, her sister and young brother were spared.

### Rebecca Dunlap

Rebecca was born on 4th June 1851 in Arkansas to parents Jesse and Mary Dunlap. Her parents and seven older siblings were killed in the massacre. Along with her two younger sisters, Rebecca was spared and taken in by Mormon follower Jacob Hamblin and his family in Santa Clara, Utah.

Two years later Rebecca and her younger sisters were able to return to Arkansas, where they were raised by their uncle James Dunlap.

In 1874 Rebecca, now an adult in her twenties, married John Wesley Evans and together they had five children. Rebecca died on 4th August 1914 in Arkansas.

## Louisa Dunlap

Louisa was born on 10th November 1853 in Arkansas, the second youngest of ten children born to Jesse and Mary Dunlap.

On 15th December 1875 she married James M Linton at Boone County and together they went on to have several children together.

Louisa died on 2nd May 1926 in Muskogee, Oklahoma.

## Sarah Elizabeth Dunlap

Sarah was born on 13th August 1856 in Arkansas to parents Jesse and Mary Dunlap.

After surviving being shot in the arm during the Mountain Meadows massacre, Sarah and her two surviving sisters - Rebecca and Louisa - were, as mentioned above, sent to live with Jacob Hamblin. Two years after this their uncle James Dunlap took the three of them back to their home state of Arkansas. Sarah grew up almost blind, which some have attributed to the attack and the lack of care she experienced in the aftermath.

US Army Captain James Lynch, who took an interest and cared about the three sisters, would often visit them as they grew up. On hearing later that Captain Lynch was ill, Sarah, by this time an adult, offered to take care of him. Lynch recovered and he and Sarah were married on 30th December 1893. At the time of the marriage James was 74 and Sarah 37. They spent the next few years together in Arkansas, where James opened his own store and Sarah taught at the local Sunday school.

Sarah died in 1901. Her husband died nine years later in 1910 and was buried next to his wife in Calhoun County, Arkansas.

## Tryphena D Fancher

In 1859, two years after the attack, 4-year-old Tryphena was happily reunited with her older brother 'Kit' Carson Fancher.

After years growing up without a family, Tryphena met and married a farmer called James Chaney Wilson. This took place on 8th July 1871 in Carroll County, Arkansas.

Tryphena died in Carroll County, Arkansas on 30th April 1897. Her husband James remarried and his new wife raised his children with Tryphena as part of her own family.

## William Twitty Baker

William was born in 1856 in Carroll County, Arkansas. He survived the Mountain Meadows massacre along with his two older sisters; his parents George and younger sister Minerva Baker did not. William would go on to marry twice and become a father of 14 children. He died in 1937 in Searcy County, Arkansas where he was buried.

---

Many years after massacre, some of the surviving children were interviewed, their stories appearing in the *Arkansas Gazette*[79] amongst other publications.

It was in 1875 that survivor Nancy Huff described in some detail her experience at the Mountain Meadows:

> I am the daughter of Peter Huff; my mother's maiden name was Salidia Brown, daughter of Alexander Brown of Tennessee . I was born in Benton county, Arkansas. in 1853. My father started to move from that county in the spring of 1857, with the ill fated train bound for California . I was then a little past four years old. I can recollect my father and mother very well, as [well as] many little incidents that occurred about that time our travels on the road, etc. I recollect passing through Salt Lake City , and passing through other places, and I recollect we were in a small prairie. One

79   A publication that ran from 1819-1991.

morning before day I was woke up by the firing of guns, and learned that our camp had been attacked, we suppose[d], by Indians. Some of the men folk were wounded. The men dug a ditch around our camp, and fortified [the camp] the best they could. The women and children got in the ditches, and were comparitively [sic] out of danger their fortifications, the attacking party went off. Soon afterward a party that we thought to be friends came up with a white flag, and said that they could protect us. They said they were our friends, and if we would come out and leave what we had they would take us to Cedar City , where we would be safe, and that they would protect us, and see that none of us were hurt. Our people agreed to this, and all started out, men, women and children, and left everything we had behind. When we had got out a short distance from the wagons, where we had been fortified, we came to a place where tall sage brush was growing on both sides of the road, and as we were passing through this place we found we were trapped, as men had hid in it, and began to shoot among us, and then rushed upon our people from both sides, killing everybody they came to. Capt. Baker had me in his arms when he was shot down, and fell dead. I saw my mother shot in the forehead and fall dead. The women and children screamed and clung together. Some of the young women begged the assassins after they had run out on us not to kill them, but they had no mercy on them, clubbing them with their guns and beating out their brains.

Some of the murderers were white men and some I supposed were Indians from their dress. At the close of the massacre there was eighteen children still alive, one girl, some ten or twelve years old, they said was too big and could tell, so they killed her, leaving seventeen. A man, I afterwards learned to be named John Willis, took me in his charge (the children were divided) and carried me to his house next day in a wagon; he lived at Cedar City and was a Mormon; he kept me there that winter. Next spring he moved to a place called Topersville [Toquerville]. I stayed there about a year, until Dr. Forney had us children gathered up and carried us to Santa Clara, from there we went to Salt Lake City and remained two months, from there we came back to the states. I know that most of the party that did the killing were white men. The Mormons got all the plunder. I saw many things afterward.

John Willis had, in his family, bed clothes, clothing, and many other things that I recognized as having belonged to my mother. When I claimed the things, they told me I was a liar, and tried to make me believe it was the Indians that killed and plundered our people, but I knew better, because I recollected seeing them kill our folks, and knew many things that they carried off that I saw in their possession afterward. I saw Willis during the massacre; he carried me off from the spot; I could not be mistaken.

Living with him made me know him beyond a doubt. I saw them shoot the girl after we were gathered up. I had a sister that was nearly grown, and four brothers that they killed. I was the youngest child of our family, the only one that was spared. They kept the children all separated whilst we remained with them. The scenes and incidents of the massacre were so terrible that they were indelibly stamped on my mind, notwithstanding I was so young at the time'.[80]

---

It is important to again state that the level of involvement of Jonathan Pugmire Sr is still unclear.

---

80   Taken from the *Arkansas Gazette*, 1st September 1875.

# 39

# THE WILL OF
# JONATHAN PUGMIRE SR

Returning back to our protagonist, it was on 11th August 1876 that the Will of Jonathan Pugmire Sr was presented into the public domain.

As with such documents, it shows us the people he was thinking about with regard to who he could and wanted to help as he entered into his older years.

What follows is the transcript of his Will.

———————————

Know all whom it may concern that I, Jonathan Pugmire of the City and County of Salt Lake and Territory of Utah, being of sound mind and memory and knowing the uncertainty of this transitory state of existance do make, publish and declare this my Last Will and Testament, that is to say: after all my just and lawful debts and liabilities shall have been paid and discharged; including the expenses of my last sickness and interment, the residue of my property and estate of whatsoever nature or kind it may be, I will, bequeath and dispose of as follows:

FIRST - To my wife, Elizabeth I will and bequeath the homestead whereon I now reside, to wit: The North West corner of Lot Five (5) Block Fifty (50) Plat "A" Salt Lake City Survey, being a piece of parcel of land seven and a half rods in width East and West by Eight and a half rods in length North and South, excepting a piece in the Southwest corner thereof, two and a half rods in width North and South by six rods East or back from the street together with all the rights and privileges thereunto belonging which my said wife is to have the exclusive control, use and occupancy thereof and enjoy all the rents, issues and profits arising therefrom, during her natural life: and after her decease, I will, bequeath and devise the said premises, occupied by me as homestead - with the exception of the piece in the South West corner thereof hereinbefore described - to my son, Jonathan Pugmire Jr. and to his heirs and assigns forever..

SECOND - It is my Will, and I so order and direct that the piece of land in the South West corner of my said homestead premises, being two and a half rods North and South by six rods East and West that is to say all my right title and equitable interest therein shall be sold and out of the means that shall be derived from such sale, it is my Will that my daughter Sarah Riley wife of Allen Riley shall be paid the sum of One Hundred Dollars; to my daughter Elizabeth Joseph, the wife of JJ Joseph, the sum of One Hundred Dollars; and to my son Joseph Pugmire, the sum of One hundred and Fifty Dollars, which sums of money shall be paid by my executor or executors to the said legatees as soon as the same shall be realized from the sale of the said premises or my interest therein - by my said executor. Should the said premises be sold for more than enough to pay the aforesaid bequests, amounting in the aggregate to Three hundred and fifty dollars, it is my Will that my said Son, Jonathan Pugmire Jr. shall receive and have the remainder after the expenses incident to the said sale shall be paid.

THIRD - To my daughter Hannah Burns I will, bequeath and devise, and to her heirs and assigns forever all my right title and interest, in and to the North half of Lot Four, Block Forty Nine, Plat "A" Salt Lake City the same being the undivided one half interest in said premises.

FOURTH - My farm, situated at or near St. Charles, Bear Lake, Idaho Territory containing about fifty acres of land, and three City lots in the Town of St. Charles owned by me, I give and bequeath to my Grandson Vincent Pugmire.

FIFTH - To my grandsons George Pugmire and James Pugmire, and Robert Pugmire and Edward Pugmire and to my Granddaughter Lizzie Pugmire I give and bequeath each one cow.

SIXTH - The residue of my estate, real and personal which I may [illegible] of or may be entitled to, at the time of my decease, not necessary for the payment of debts, liabilities and charges against my said estate, I give and bequeath to my grandchildren, the sons and daughters of my said son Jonathan Pugmire Jr., that may then be living share and share alike.

SEVENTH - I hereby nominate and appoint Samuel Bennion and Henry Dinwoodey to be the Executor of this my Last Will and Testament, hereby revoking all other Wills that may have been by me made.

In witness whereof I hereunto set my hand, and seal at Salt Lake City this 26th day of July A.D. 1876

/s/ Jonathan Pugmire (seal)

Signed, Sealed and published and declared by the said Jonathan Pugmire to be his last Will and Testament in our presence, and at his request we sign our names as witnesses hereto. The day and year last above written.

/s/ William Cooper Residing in Salt Lake City

/s/ Silas T. Smith same.[81]

Jonathan had clearly done rather well for himself. As his Will shows, he had money, property and livestock – no doubt a relief to him in his last days, knowing that he could provide a future for his children and his children's children.

---

81  Taken from 'Pioneers and Prominent Men of Utah, Church Chronology and History'.

# 40

# THE PUGMIRE CHILDREN

The following chapter takes a more detailed look at Jonathan Pugmire Sr's children, and what became of them following his death in Salt Lake City, Utah.

---

There were twelve children in all, although it would not be unreasonable to suggest that there may have been more that were not recorded.

George Pugmire (1821-1868)

Jonathan Pugmire Jr (1823-1880)

Sarah Pugmire (1826-1902)

Richard Pugmire (1828-1839)

Joseph Pugmire (1830-1830)

Joseph Hyrum Pugmire (1833-1906)

William Pugmire (1836-1837)

Elizabeth Pugmire (1837-1911)

John Pugmire (1840-1852)

Hannah Pugmire (1842-1931)

Moroni Pugmire (1846-1846)

Mary Ann Pugmire (1853-1910)

## George Pugmire

George Pugmire was born in the north of England in 1821, and was the first born and eldest son of Jonathan Pugmire Sr and Elizabeth Barnes.

Twenty years later, in 1841, 20-year-old George Pugmire married Jane Russell in Liverpool. In 1844, as the family headed for new pastures overseas, George chose not to relocate and so remained in Liverpool.

He died in 1868 in Liverpool at the age of 45. His wife Jane died seven years later in 1875. No records exist to show they had any children together.

### Jonathan Pugmire Jr.

Jonathan Jr was born on 7th December 1823 in Carlisle, Cumberland, and grew up learning the work of the blacksmith as taught to him by his father. Whilst travelling to America with his family in 1844 aboard the *Isaac Allerton,* he met and fell in love with a young Scottish convert to Mormonism from Dunbartonshire called Elizabeth McKay (1822-1887). They married on 30th April 1844 in Nauvoo, Illinois. Following the marriage Jonathan Jr went on to serve as part of the Nauvoo Legion and plied his trade for many years as a blacksmith.

In 1868 he relocated to St Charles, Idaho, where he continued his blacksmith work and set up a farm of his own. He practiced polygamy and found himself with three different families.

He died unexpectedly on 18th September 1880 at St Charles in Bear Lake County, Idaho. Following this, his wives and their children decided to live together.

### Sarah Pugmire

The eldest daughter was born on 28th March 1826 in Carlisle, Cumberland and was christened into the Church of England in March of the same year. She went on to marry a man named Allen F Riley and together they had at least two children. Sarah died on 31st October 1902 in Salt Lake City, Utah and was buried on 3rd November 1902.

### Richard Pugmire

Richard Pugmire was born on 21st September 1828 in Liverpool, and died there on 24th October 1839 aged just 11.

### Joseph Pugmire

Joseph Pugmire was born in 1830 but sadly did not live long

enough to experience a life.

### Joseph Hyrum Pugmire

Joseph Hyrum Pugmire was born on 26th August 1833 in Liverpool and travelled with his parents and siblings to a new life in America when he was 11-years-old.

On 5th October 1855 he married Eleanor Creighton in Cedar City, Utah and records show that together they had eleven children. On 29th June 1887 he married Martha Ashworth in Cache, Utah.

Joseph died at Salem, Fremont, Idaho on 20th November 1906.

### William Pugmire

William was born in England in 1836, and tragically died almost immediately after his birth.

### Elizabeth Pugmire

Jonathan's second daughter Elizabeth was born in England in 1834. Travelling with her parents to America in 1844 she would go on to marry three times, first to Jesse Benjamin Lewis in 1846 in Illinois. Following this she married Judah Jacob Joseph in 1865 in California, and later went on to marry a man called Mortimer G. Taylor. Elizabeth died in 1911 in Utah.

### John Pugmire

John Pugmire was born in Liverpool on 14th May 1840 and emigrated with his family when he was 4-years-old. On 2nd January 1852, when not yet 12 years of age, John Pugmire was shot and killed by a young man called Jerome Owen whilst they were herding cattle together near the city of Parowan, Utah.

### Hannah Pugmire

Hannah Pugmire was born on 11th September 1842 in Lancashire and died on 31st August 1931 in Los Angeles,

California. She married several times and had four children with husbands Edward Hope, Beverly C. Boren and George W. Heimer.

## Moroni Pugmire

Moroni Pugmire was born on 20th April 1846 in Montrose, Iowa and according to records sadly only lived for one day.

## Mary Ann Pugmire

The daughter of Jonathan Pugmire Sr and his second wife Mary Baylis Haywood, Mary Ann was born in April 1853 in Beaver County, Utah. She went on to marry Peter D Chambers and together they had nine children. Mary died on 25th October 1910 in Salt Lake, Utah.

---

Many of the descendents of the Pugmire family are still alive in Utah State today. How much they know of their ancestry is not known.

---

# CONCLUSION

So there you have it, an extraordinary story of a man from northern England born at the very beginning of the nineteenth century who trained as a blacksmith in the quiet countryside.

A man who moved from his home and utilised his trade by working for the nearby railway.

A curious man who, becoming aware of the arrival of Mormon missionaries, was converted and became a member of The Church of Jesus Christ of Latter Day Saints.

The man who, excited by his discovery of a new faith, converted his friend who was also his work colleague, and then attempted to convert the wife of this friend, which resulted in a terrible drowning.

This was the man who was tried for manslaughter.

This was the man who left England with his family on a voyage that would take weeks across the seas to begin a new life in America.

A man who arrived just as the leader of the religious movement he became part of was about to be shot and killed.

This was the story of the man who lost his wife to the winter and a son to a bullet, and yet still continued on.

This man helped new settlers to feel welcome.

This was a man who was involved in the infamous historical events that took place in the Mountain Meadows in Utah, America.

This was a man who believed.

This was the true story of Mr Jonathan Pugmire Sr.

———————————

# SELECTED BIBLIOGRAPHY
# AND SOURCES

## Books

Backus, Anna Jean, *Mountain Meadows Witness: The Life and Times of Bishop Philip Klingensmith* (Spokane: Arthur H. Clark, 1995)

Bigler, David L. and Will Bagley (eds.), *Innocent Blood: Essential Narratives of the Mountain Meadows Massacre* (Spokane: Arthur H. Clark, 2008)

Birney, Hoffman, *Zealots of Zion* (Philadelphia: Penn Publishing Co., 1931)

Brooks, Juanita, *The Mountain Meadows Massacre* (Stanford University Press, 1950)

——— (ed.), *Journal of the Southern Indian Mission: Diary of Thomas D. Brown* (Logan: Utah State University Press, 1972)

Bushman, Richard, *Joseph Smith: Rough Stone Rolling* (New York: Alfred A. Knopf, 2005)

Carter, Kate B., *Heart Throbs of the West* (Salt Lake City: Daughters of Utah Pioneers, 1947)

Flanders, Robert B., *Nauvoo: Kingdom on the Mississippi* (University of Illinois, 1975)

Givens, George W., *500 More Little Known Facts In Mormon History* (Springville, Utah: Bonneville Books, 2004)

Jenkins, Ryan C, *The Assassination of Joseph Smith: Innocent Blood on the Banner of Liberty* (Springville, Utah: Cedar Fort, Inc, 2014)

Jones, Evelyn K., *Henry Lunt Biography* (Lulu.com, 2014)

Nelson, Lee, *The Journal of Joseph, The Personal History of a Modern Prophet* (Mapleton, Utah, 1979)

Shirts, Morris A. and Kathryn H. Shirts, *A Trial Furnace: South Southern Utah's Iron Mission* (Brigham Young University Press, 2001)

Walker, Ronald W., Richard E. Turley, and Glen M. Leonard, *Massacre at Mountain Meadows* (Oxford University Press, 2008)

Wilde, Elaine Genevieve Pugmire and Cheryl Wilde Crowther, *Be Thou Humble: Insight Into the Life of Jonathan Pugmire Senior* (Independently published, 2015) (ISBN: 9781505672381)

**Other Sources**

*Elders' Journal of the Church of Latter Day Saints* (ed. Carlos Smith)

*History of the Church of Jesus Christ of Latter-day Saints, The* (in seven volumes)

*Oxford English Dictionary*

**Censuses**

1850 Census: Great Salt Lake, Utah Territory (M432 Roll 919 p.50)

1850 Census: Iron County, Utah Territory (M432 Roll 919 p. 23)

1860 Census: Great Salt Lake, Utah (M653 Roll 1313 p.117)

1870 Census: Salt Lake City, Utah (M593 Roll 1611 p.584)

---

# INDEX